主编: 孙向晨、龚彦
联合主办: 上海当代艺术博物馆、复旦大学哲学学院

实录

ECP Charging
Station
Workshop Series:
Curating and
Philosophy of Art

Record

Edited by Sun Xiangchen, Gong Yan
Co-organizers: Power Station of Art,
School of Philosophy, Fudan University

上海三聯書店

图书在版编目（CIP）数据

青策充电站：策展与艺术哲学工作坊 / 孙向晨，龚
彦主编 . – 上海：上海三联书店，2021.5
ISBN 978-7-5426-7276-6

Ⅰ.①青… Ⅱ.①孙… ②龚… Ⅲ.①艺术－展览会
－策划－研究 Ⅳ.① G245

中国版本图书馆 CIP 数据核字（2020）第241218号

青策充电站：策展与艺术哲学工作坊

主　　编：孙向晨　龚　彦

责任编辑：殷亚平
特约编辑：甯　佳（上海当代艺术博物馆）
　　　　　马慧婷（上海当代艺术博物馆）
装帧设计：邵君瑜（上海当代艺术博物馆）
监　　制：姚　军
责任校对：王凌霄

出版发行：上海三联书店
　　　　　（200030）中国上海市漕溪北路331号 A 座6楼
邮购电话：021-22895540
印　　刷：上海普顺印刷包装有限公司

版　　次：2021年5月第1版
印　　次：2021年5月第1次印刷
开　　本：787mm×1092mm　1/32
字　　数：250千字
印　　张：9.125
书　　号：ISBN 978-7-5426-7276-6/G·1585
定　　价：98.00 元

敬启读者，如发现本书有印装质量问题，请与印刷厂联系021-36522998

序

复旦大学哲学学院院长　孙向晨

2020年1月，复旦大学在哲学学院内成立了艺术哲学系，这是中国第一家艺术哲学系，这背后饱含着我们对于艺术与哲学的真切关注。

早在2018年，复旦大学哲学学院就与上海当代艺术博物馆合作展开了第12届上海双年展"禹步"的开幕论坛，2020年开幕的第13届上海双年展"水体"，上海当代艺术博物馆再度与复旦大学哲学学院合作，进行了跨界的双年展开幕论坛。在艺术家与哲学家的一次次合作中，有相互的欣赏，相互的激荡，也有相互的交锋。艺术与哲学，现代世界寻求自由的两股力量，一起构成了上海当代艺术的一种新面向。因此，我们在"青年策展人"培养上的合作——"青策充电站：策展与艺术哲学工作坊"——便也顺理成章。复旦大学哲学学院的沈语冰老师、张双利老师以及后来加盟复旦哲学的鲁明军老师，都在"青策充电站"工作坊上举行了非常深入的讲座。这是一次非常有效的、充满活力的合作，不仅深受学员们的欢迎，也获得了"2019年度全国美术馆优秀公共教育项目"的称号。

哲学与艺术看似离得遥远，哲学是远离感性的理论学科，有着高度的逻辑与概念的要求，艺术则是最为感性直观的，始终离不开对象的呈现，无论是具象的还是抽象的。两件非常远离的工作，事实上却有着极大的热忱，希望能够相互走近。

艺术有强烈的自主性，艺术创造从来无需哲学的介入，把握一件艺术作品也无需哲学的反思；另一方面，任何一个大哲学家大概都不会忽视人类生存图景中艺术的存在，柏拉图如此，黑格尔如此，海德格尔更是如此。艺术家不管其本人如何思想，如何构思，不管艺术创造多么具有个性，多么别具一格，艺术品之为艺术品，从来不是一件私人"物品"，"作品"在艺术史上的地位离不开某种哲学式的思考。艺术批评理论与哲学有着千丝万缕的关系，每一位艺术批评理论家的背后都站着不同的哲学家，抑或有些哲学家开始直接面对艺术作品。张双利老师讲的文化工业理论，沈语冰老师讲的艺术批评理论以及鲁明军老师的策展主题，无不与哲学思考息息相关；其他讲者的内容也都可以引申到哲学层面上来讨论，正如孙原先生所说，策展人除了第一、二阶的知识，还需要第三阶的知识；翁子健先生讲的"展览史的本体问题"以及比利安娜·思瑞克女士还原上海当年展览的知识生产过程都可以深入到哲学层面来讨论。策展与艺术哲学有着内在的关联。

美学固然是哲学的分支领域，但哲学绝不能只是抽象地谈论美，抽象地谈论艺术；哲学必须有能力自己来面对艺术作品，以哲学的方式来直面具有哲学意义的作品。当代艺术作品也远不是一个"美"字所能涵盖，其意涵深远得多。因此，艺术哲学首先是一个如何让哲学来面对艺术的问题。

就我所理解的艺术与哲学，最为直接的关联可以概括为五个层面：首先是艺术中直接呈现出的哲学家与哲学主题，一种可视化的哲学形象。最著名的莫过于拉斐尔的《雅典学院》，夏丹尔的《哲学》，大卫的《苏格拉底之死》，还有高更的《我们从哪里来，我们是谁，我们往何处去》，基里柯的《伟大的形而上学家》等；其二是艺术与哲学之间的类比性，研究艺术史的学者经常会提到普桑与笛卡尔哲学的关系，不仅是他们生活在同一个时代，而是他们在思想上、在精神上有某种类似性，诸如此类的还有库尔贝与实证主义，莫奈与休谟，塞尚与康德等；其三是艺术自身的发展所提出的哲学性问题，比如图像与观念之间的关系，图像反映观念？抑或图像自身作为观念？对现代艺术来说，在杜尚之后追求图像的绘画何以可能？现成品与艺术品的关系究竟为何？艺术是否已经终结？其四是艺术在人类生存中的位置，如海德格尔对梵高的分析乃至阿多诺、本雅明对艺术在现代社会的批判；其五则是最为根本性的，在中西方艺术背后的本体论预设，为什么西方古典艺术传统总是不断地追求"真实"，而苏轼所代表的文人画却说"论画以形似，见与儿童邻"，看似艺术风格的不同，背后有着强烈的不同哲学预设。凡此种种，艺术与哲学之间有着丰富的关联，而艺术作品之于哲学的意义就是由艺术与哲学之间不同的关系所决定。在策展活动中，这些问题会变得特别突出。

必须承认，艺术史面对作品与哲学面对作品是完全不同的。最著名案例就是夏皮罗对于海德格尔评论梵高的批评以及德里达对夏皮罗的反批评。事实上，哲学有其自身理由来面对作品，这会深刻地影响我们对于艺术意义的理解，也会影响我们策展的思路。现代艺术的创作有其自主性，但其意义的生成却有别于艺术的创作。哲学不需要去现场侵扰艺术的自主创作，但现代艺术的意义生成机制却总也离不开哲学的在场。

在这个意义上，我们所说的艺术哲学本质上并不是一种Philosophy of Art，而是Art·Philosophy；一个"of"就有了哲学对于艺术的某种"概括"，这不是哲学该有的企图心；哲学与艺术的关系本质上是一种"艺术·哲学"。这之间的"点"尤为重要，一是以这个"点"表明两者处于两个世界，概念的世界与感性的世界，各有自己的生命力；另一方面，这个"点"又把两者如此拉近，使之能够相互照面，相互对话。

"青策充电站"以其独特的姿态置身于艺术与哲学之间，那个"之间"的"点"也许正是策展人的内在使命。感谢与上海当代艺术博物馆的合作，感谢与上海当代艺术博物馆龚彦馆长的合作，希望继续携手，创造出别样的未来。

是为序。

序

上海当代艺术博物馆馆长　龚彦

2020年1月18—20日，正当""2019青策计划"展览和"青策充电站"公共教育项目在上海当代艺术博物馆举行之际，在热闹的展厅和鲜活的课堂之外，一场疫情正在蛰伏。

很快，整个社会为冠状病毒困扰。2020年春节之际，上海当代艺术博物馆第一时间停止对公众开放，何时恢复待定。

没有观众的电厂空空荡荡的，卸下了人流数据的压力，像是回到了出生时的样子。一楼大厅，"2019青策计划"的展厅外墙仿佛一束高光，喷射而出的彩纸悬停在空中，提示着人们这场欢庆尚未结束。

作品在没有观众的展厅里喃喃自语或相互交谈，这并不妨碍我们去感受青年策展人最大限度地追求自己向往的生活的决心。展厅仿佛诺齐克描述的"最小国家"，一个乌托邦的框架，我们不带预设地观赏正义、公平、权力、过程、主客关系。观者的缺失让展览释放出了异样的能量，让我们突然意识到，面对和发现世界的方式其实只剩下了一种——告别。告别药剂，告别滞后，告别观念。

我们不能回到古典，艺术不能只代表过去或者未来，除了训诫和希望，它还要让我们看到无知。我们要对学术圈里的"当下"充满怀疑。面对活生生的、触目惊心的图像和谎言，"社会介入"和"研究性创作"已如花拳绣腿。"当代"艺术的"滞后"让它的制造者们露出了投机的尾巴：因为滞后，艺术才得以成为产品。所以某种程度，参加"青年策展人计划"的策展人、艺术家、讲者和青年学员们是孤独的，或许他们能信任的只有生命本身，尼采已经戴着虚无的口罩潜入人群。

一场流行病提醒我们鼠疫、霍乱、麻风……那些肉眼看不见的病毒随时会披上另一件外套潜入城市，瓦解城市，改写人类的历史。现代城市的脆弱和被动如同它形成的法则，是时候思考另一种城市系统了。当代艺术何尝不是，策展又何尝不是呢？

"青策计划2019"在展期（2019年10月25日—2020年3月29日）内推出的"青策充电站"项目，由上海当代艺术博物馆与复旦大学学院携手邀请世界范围内当代艺术与哲学领域的资深实践者、学者集中开讲，以多维度的视角及敏锐的前沿研究为青年策展人提供理论与实践的经验支持，开启思辨的实验与碰撞。"青策充电站"项目的出版工作大多是在2020年疫情下的特殊状态中完成的，它希冀将节庆式的展览演变为对青年策展人生长需求的助力。"生长"本身并不属于一年里的某个特殊日子，而是属于生命所持续的时时刻刻。

感谢孙向晨院长和复旦哲学学院对当代艺术的热忱，艺术与哲学、美术馆与学院对话，将让我们共同前进，让更多的年轻人脱颖而出！

关于"青年策展人计划"与"青策充电站"项目

上海当代艺术博物馆的"青年策展人计划"是国内目前独树一帜的青年策展人发展与研究项目,自2014年创立至今已推出三十余位年轻策展人,并助力他们实现了十六场展览。作为上海当代艺术博物馆的年度展览品牌暨学术品牌,"青年策展人计划"致力于发掘华人青年策展力量,为他们提供实践理想的平台、全面且深度的指导、进入公共视野的途径和良性的成长环境。

"青年策展人计划"迎来六周年之际,上海当代艺术博物馆携手在人文艺术理论研究领域具有引领性优势的复旦大学哲学学院,于"青策计划2019"展期内联合推出"青策充电站"项目,邀请世界范围内当代艺术与哲学领域的资深实践者、学者集中开讲,以多维度的视角及敏锐的前沿研究为青年策展人提供理论与实践的经验支持,开启思辨的实验与碰撞。

About Emerging Curators Project (ECP) and ECP Charging Station Programme

Emerging Curators Project (ECP) hosted by Power Station of Art (PSA) is China's exclusive young curator development and research project. Since its foundation in 2014, ECP has so far supported more than 30 Chinese curatorial talents to realize a total of 16 exhibitions. As PSA's annual exhibitory and academic trademark, the project stays committed to exploring young Chinese curatorial talents and providing them with a platform to practice conceptions, an opportunity to access comprehensive and in-depth guidance, a path to enter the public's eyes, and an environment to enjoy healthy growth.

Upon the sixth anniversary of ECP, PSA in collaboration with the School of Philosophy, Fudan University, the leading institution with significant advantage in the research field of humanities and arts, jointly present the "ECP Charging Station" programme during the exhibition of ECP 2019. The programme invites senior practitioners and scholars in the fields of contemporary art and philosophy around the world to give lectures intensively. With multidimensional perspectives and keen cutting-edge researches, "ECP Charging Station" aims at providing support for theoretical and practical experience for emerging curators and opening up experiments and clashes of ideas.

青策充电站
联合主办：上海当代艺术博物馆、复旦大学哲学学院

工作团队
上海当代艺术博物馆：张琍莉、马慧婷、徐辰斐、邱鼎、黄彦娜
复旦大学哲学学院：袁新、林晖、沈奇岚、陈佳

实录册编辑团队
主编：孙向晨、龚彦
编辑：马慧婷、蔺佳
平面设计：邵君瑜
翻译：曾晨
校对：阮汇善

ECP Charging Station Programme
Co-organizers: Power Station of Art,
School of Philosophy, Fudan University

Programme Team
Power Station of Art: Zhang Lili, Ma Huiting, Xu Chenfei,
Qiu Ding, Huang Yanna
School of Philosophy, Fudan University: Yuan Xin, Lin Hui,
Shen Qilan, Chen Jia

Editorial Team
Editor: Sun Xiangchen, Gong Yan, Ma Huiting, Lin Jia
Graphic Design: Shao Junyu
Translator: Zen Chen
Proofreader: Ruan Huishan

青策充电站
策展与艺术哲学
工作坊

实录

ECP Charging
Station
Workshop Series:
Curating and
Philosophy of Art

Record

由于"艺术家""策展人"是两个流变的概念,他们之间的关系一定是不确定的并且一直在发生变化的。围绕这个题目希望讨论以下问题:艺术家会经历哪些不同阶段?艺术家在面对艺术时的思考方式与策展人有什么不同?他们各自的思考起点、身份焦虑是怎样的?今天的艺术家与策展人,与过去相比发生了哪些变化?今天的艺术家在什么程度上需要策展人?哪一类的艺术家需要哪一类的策展人?艺术家希望策展人变得更怎样一些,策展人希望艺术家变得更怎样一些,或者策展人跟艺术家怎样才能一块儿更怎样一些?

孙原：
艺术家需要
策展人吗？

作为"艺术家"的艺术家：艺术有一个好处，就是不需要正确

大家好，我是孙原，我今天要讲的题目是"艺术家需要策展人吗？"。我的自我定位是"艺术家"，我其实不太懂哲学。我觉得哲学和艺术的关系或许有点类似精神病学和精神病人的关系——研究学问需要研究对象。我其实觉得自己不太有资格给大家讲课，今天我坐在这里或许对于学习艺术和哲学的朋友们来说更像是一个研究对象，大家也可以观察我。我说的内容不一定对，但艺术有一个好处，就是不需要正确。当然，如果你们对我讲的内容有疑问或者质疑就随时讨论，咱们可以互相指教。

2019年，我在参加威尼斯双年展的时候顺便前往了佛罗伦萨和罗马的美术学院做讲座，借此机会也和从国内过去学习艺术的青年留学生进行了交流。交流的过程中，我发现了一个问题，这些学习艺术的年轻人（其中很多人学的是当代艺术）特别希望能够了解艺术到底是怎么一回事儿。他们在西方古典艺术的发源地学习，似乎离艺术很近，但是又搞不懂，感觉就像隔着一层窗户纸。他们提出的问题都挺简单，我能感觉到他们在学习的过程中缺乏一种创造性思维。实际上，学艺术并不是学成之

后才成为艺术家开始创作，而是在学习的过程中就要创造出方法，这个方法不一定对，但它能够帮助到自己。一个对的东西往往没什么用，真理就是一句很正确的废话。无论是作为艺术家进行创作、还是作为策展人策划展览，或者作为学者来撰写评论、研究艺术，大都是在通过创造某种方法去思考一件事。

我为大家准备了三个作品的视频。第一个是我和彭禹2019年参展威尼斯双年展的作品《难自禁》图示1，P6&P7，这个短片还原了布展的过程。2016年，这件作品曾经在古根海姆美术馆完成过一次，其实最早的想法是让一个机器人不停地工作，机器人会以机械臂阻止地面上的液体向外流动。刚开始我们不希望采用这种把它封闭在一个玻璃柜里的展示方式，但是机器人的力量非常大、速度也快，美术馆要求作品必须跟人隔离，防止有人会走到机器跟前受到伤害。所以，最后这件作品展出时就整个被玻璃圈起来，等于它在一个车间式的透明封闭空间里工作。地上的液体是一种可食用的增稠剂，加上了色素。它的基本原理就像是瓶子倒了后，水流到桌面上，你会下意识地用手去阻挡水的流向，暂时把水圈在一个安全范围内，防止它流到地上。这件作品就是通过一个可以来回转的、机械臂前端带刮板的机器不停地工作，将周围的液体控制在一个范围里。

这是我和彭禹在威尼斯参展的另外一件作品《亲爱的》图示2，P8。

2013年，我们在乌克兰基辅的平丘克艺术中心有一个项目《当看不再是一个选择》图示3，P9，我们在艺术中心里做了一个训练基地，训练武器使用。最初我们希望邀请国内的人去那里参与，但是在实现上遇到了许多困难，最终我们决定在乌克兰当地征集志愿者。当地人的参与热情非常高，报名的人很多，最终有18名志愿者通过政审参加了这个训练项目。主要的训练内容是参与者蒙着眼睛拆装武器，这个过程由专业的部队教官来指导。

训练了一个星期后，大部分人能够在一分多钟的时间里完成一次拆装。每周四还有一节课是由乌克兰的武器专家教授各种武器的使用方法。这个训练营计划持续半年，但是实际上只持续了几个月，这样的项目能在美术馆里实现还是不太容易的，主办方也是向政府申请后获得批准，而且还在美术馆里建了一个大笼子。出于安全考虑，所有想要体验这件作品的观众都得先检查护照，并完成登记。这个计划完成之后大概过了半年的时间，乌克兰就发生革命了，展览举办地附近广场上的列宁像被推倒了。当然这不是我们造成的。但是革命发生后我突然能理解为什么当地很多人有热情去报名参加这个训练项目，就是他们有这样一种渴望。我觉得还挺有意思的吧，这是一种契合。

作为"策展人"的艺术家：不在图像中行动

作品创作之外，我也策划过展览。五年前我在北京的三个比较大的艺术空间(常青画廊、佩斯画廊、唐人当代艺术中心)策划过一个名为"不在图像中行动"的展览图示4，P10&P11。这个展览并不是一个即兴的展览。

现在的展览方式很多，有一些自我组织式的，或是带有某种命题式的，比较即兴的，还有一些可以在公共媒体平台上通过非常轻盈、小规模的方式呈现。当初我在构思这个展览时，围绕展览方式思考了很长时间。其实我年轻的时候对艺术挺感兴趣的，我愿意看展览，也愿意去参加展览。当时我就住在北京798园区里面，那儿每天都发生很多展览，一周几十次开幕。我看了一段时间后就再也不看任何展览了。在很多年里，中国的年轻艺术家，他们呈现出一种越做越像当代艺术的艺术——首先是他们很会做装置，也很会布展，作品里大量使用了影像和现成品，极具抽象感；作品的制作感和完成度都具有今天的当代艺术的样子。当时我就觉得，这种作品跟艺术家之间有什

1.

孙原 & 彭禹作品《难自禁》于 2019年威尼斯双年展现场。图 片由艺术家提供。© 孙原 & 彭 禹工作室

Installation view of *Can't Help Myself* by Sun Yuan & Peng Yu at the Venice Biennale 2019. Image courtesy of the artists. © Sun Yuan & Peng Yu Studio

2.

孙原 & 彭禹作品《亲爱的》于
2019年威尼斯双年展现场。图
片由艺术家提供。© 孙原 & 彭
禹工作室

Installation view of *Dear* by Sun Yuan
& Peng Yu at the Venice Biennale 2019.
Image courtesy of the artists. © Sun
Yuan & Peng Yu Studio

3.

孙原 & 彭禹作品《当看不再是一种选择》，基辅平丘克艺术中心，乌克兰，2013。图片由艺术家提供。© 孙原 & 彭禹工作室

If Seeing Is Not an Option by Sun Yuan & Peng Yu, Pinchuk Art Center, Kyir Ukraine, 2013. Image courtesy of the artists. © Sun Yuan & Peng Yu Studio

4.

"不在图像中行动"展览现场，
图片由艺术家提供。© 孙原 &
彭禹工作室

Installation view of "Unlived by What is
Seen". Image courtesy of *HiArt*. Image
courtesy of the artists. © Sun Yuan &
Peng Yu Studio

么关系？假设这个世界上没有画廊、美术馆，也没有当代艺术这件事，你到底是干什么的？你会搞这个现成品吗？你会把桌、板凳、电线放在一个展厅里面，然后起一个名字，你会干这件事吗？我特别怀疑这一点，就是艺术家到底是干什么的。我们每天都在做艺术、做展览，也不思考自己为什么要做，做它是为什么，好像仅仅就是因为自己上过艺术院校。此外，今天的当代艺术似乎不做现成品就不算搞当代，不做多媒体就不算是今天的艺术。我对这些挺有疑问的，所以我也找了一些艺术家来了解。

当时有一群艺术家聚集在一个叫黑桥艺术区的地方，我了解到他们在做的东西，有的不是很成熟，但是我的目的也不是为了让他们展现成熟。我们觉得他们应该展示"在生活中进行的有趣尝试"，未必是作品。展览大概有三十几位(组)艺术家参展，最后采取了一个统一的方法，让每位艺术家用一个视频来讲述自己干了什么。如果艺术家有证据，或者做了什么东西也可以搬来展出。但是它的目的不在于这些文献或做了什么"作品"。这个展览里也包括了李永斌、赵半狄在内的艺术家，我觉得他们具有一种类似的状态。

这个展览在当时还是反响挺大的，很多年轻的艺术家前来观展，也受到影响，并给了我许多反馈。但我觉得这个展览的主要作用还是让大家反思艺术的目的是什么。虽然展览过后，这些艺术家好像并没有沿着这条路走下去，有些又去做那种当代艺术，我觉得挺可惜的。但是，是不是这种形式一定要在很多艺术家的创作当中去延续？其实我觉得没必要。像这样的展览，它就是让艺术家退出自己的人设，回到一种基本的原始的状态中去。在一个艺术家他整个的艺术生涯里面，无论你对他有一个什么样的启发或是联想，你最终提示的可能是不要忘记艺术里面最重要的东西，而不是让他去延续某一种形式和方法。

艺术家 VS 策展人

回到今天的题目，艺术家肯定需要策展人，但是艺术家需要跟策展人一块儿干什么，怎样配合？在这里我们集中讨论的是学术意义上的策展人，而不仅仅是能找到钱、找到资源的策展人，后者更类似于电影制片人的角色，很大程度上他们在做的是行政工作。当所谓"独立策展人"这一身份出现后，他和艺术之间是什么关系？艺术家和这类策展人之间会形成怎样的交流？

简单说来我认为可以分为两大类，一种是总结型的，另一种是共同生产型的，这两种工作方法并不分高下，有的纯粹一些，也有的类似这次"青策计划"中张营营的展览，既有总结性也带有生产性。共同生产型的策展，往往艺术家还没做作品，或者还没做出策展人想要的作品，这时策展人的工作会为艺术家提示路径或者帮助他实现创作。在这种共同生产的过程中，比较不理想的方式是命题创作，比较理想的方式是艺术家能够在策展人的介入下退出自己的既有人设，去尝试一个新的方向。

艺术家和策展人都作为知识的生产者，两者间的区别在哪里？我认为根本在于他们在知识阶梯上所处的位置不一样：艺术家处在初阶阶段，决定知识如何出现，他生产的是私有知识，面对的是"无"；策展人处在一阶知识的生产阶段，他不生产私有知识，而是关注到了艺术家在生产的这个事实，他在触及私有知识的基础上决定了一阶知识如何出现，因此策展人生产的知识不是私有化的，是与艺术家共有的。

当代出现的独立策展人，在关注艺术家的同时也注意到其他人对艺术家的关注，这就相当于策展人的"策"不但是在策划这个艺术家，同时也在针对其他策展人产生某种策略；在给这个艺术家定位的同时，也在与其他的定位方式进行区别。以上可以理解为策展人进入了二阶知识的生产阶段，在这个阶段我们可以看到一个策展人的特殊性。

处于三阶的策展人还会进一步思考历史性的维度：我做的事情在艺术史或展览史的发展进程里意味着什么？这个想法是否曾经在艺术史上出现过？对将来的艺术现象或线索是否会构成重要的影响？如果这个想法曾经出现过，或者它像对之后的艺术脉络构似乎不成重要影响，这个时候还做不做？这是需要策展人思考的一个维度，也能够由此评判策展人够不够优秀。

当然，知识生产处在一阶、二阶还是三阶的位置并不直接决定策展的优劣，具体还得看在这一阶段生产的知识是否有效。类似地，艺术家也需要知道同时代的艺术家在做什么、需要考虑历史维度——但不是绝对的——只埋头考虑私有知识生产的艺术家也存在。这里仍然说到艺术家和策展人的根本性区别，即便二者对于知识的生产都处在三阶的位置，艺术家的生产归根结底还是私有知识。那么对于艺术家而言，什么时候需要策展人的介入？需要哪种介入方式？我说得功利一些，只有当策展人处在与艺术家不同的知识台阶上，这个时候策展人的介入才是特别有价值的。

我们注意到许多个展的策划，如果艺术家自己的总结梳理能力强一些，他其实根本不需要策展人的角色；很多的双年展或者官方机构举办的群展，只是简单地进行命题归类，没有生产任何比艺术家的创作本身更高一阶的知识，这个时候策展人和艺术家处在同一阶知识水平上，跟艺术家自己介绍自己也没有区别。策展人介入艺术家工作的时候，至少应当具备了一阶或二阶的知识，也就是认识到艺术家的价值，同时看到其他艺术家在做什么，甚至看到其他策展人怎么评价这个艺术家，最后相应采取了什么对策。而一个拥有三阶知识的策展人对于艺术家而言就像是电影监制的角色，他可以在艺术家沉浸于私有生产的时候去提醒或提升他的问题意识和表达策略，甚至直接影响艺术家去跳脱出既有人设，去尝试全新的、不同的路径。

我刚才说得很抽象，为了把这事儿说得尽量清楚一些，可以举一些具体的例子。今年"青策计划"里张营营的展览，王鲁炎之前也提到过它与"当态度成为形式"这个展览的关联性。为什么说1969年哈罗德·泽曼（Harald Szeemann）策划的这个展览很重要，公认的一点是哈罗德·泽曼在这个展览里确立了"独立策展人"的身份和工作方式。作为一个艺术家，我看到这个展览的特点是，展览里艺术家所呈现的个体特征并不是那么强，如果你把作品的作者名单打乱或互换似乎也成立，每一位艺术家都没有走出个人叙事那一步。还有一个特点是，这个展览结束后，很多的艺术家并没有以此为出发点继续在同一方向上发展。比如，大家所熟知的奥登伯格（Claes Oldenburg）在这个展览里展出的装置作品^{图示5, P15}，和他之后波普化的雕塑语言是完全断裂的。哈罗德·泽曼作为这个展览的号召者，将当时还是一群毛头小伙的、未来的艺术大师们聚集在一起，通过这个展览来反对当时已经僵化的形式主义、抽象表现主义，他促成了这样一种局面：所有的艺术家，无论是已经有了成熟的人设（如博伊斯），还是正在探索自己的道路，在这个展览里都退回到了一个非常基础的界面上，并且在这个基础的界面上，艺术家们完成了一次非常同质性的探索^{图示6, P15}。为了反对当时已经僵化的抽象表现主义、极简主义以及走向文字主义的概念艺术，反对这些一开始为了推翻艺术形式所采取的强硬手段的过快形式化，策展人泽曼在这里提供了一个说法——"活在脑子里"，通过一个空间——伯尔尼美术馆。比起实体意义上的展示空间，我认为泽曼在这里是为艺术家提供了一个思考的起点，一个"无"的空间。艺术家也马上采取了相应的行动去呼应他的号召，他们使用最少的、最初级化的材料去生产作品。值得注意的是，在这个阶段

5.

奥登伯格在展览"当态度成为形式"中展出的装置作品。摄影：Siegfried Kuhn © StAAG/RBA

Installation view of Claes Oldenburg's work at the exhibition "When Attitudes Become Form", 1969. Photo: Siegfried Kuhn © StAAG/RBA

6.

从左至右：约瑟夫·博伊斯，比尔·博林格尔与基斯·索尼尔在"当态度成为形式"展览现场，伯尔尼美术馆，1969。摄影：Shunk Kender © Roy Lichtenstein Foundation

From left to right: Joseph Beuys, Bill Bollinger and Keith Sonnier, "When Attitudes Become Form", Kunsthalle Bern, 1969. Photo: Shunk Kender © Roy Lichtenstein Foundation

激浪派已经开始使用电视机这样"时髦"的电器进行创作，而泽曼和艺术家在这个展览里回归到了更原始的材料。

我试图去分析在这个展览中艺术家呈现出一种同质性趋势的原因。假设整个艺术史的发展是在一个巨大的封闭空间内进行，这个空间内没有电也没有光，只有一扇窗。最初所有的艺术家都聚拢在唯一的窗口前，试图表现自己从窗口里看到的东西。后来有人发现，如果把窗户擦干净一些就能观察得更清楚一些，画得更立体。再后来有人利用光学原理更好地提高明锐度和分辨率，玻璃被换成透镜、广角镜，又有人通过光的折射看到更多色彩。逐渐地，艺术家们不再满足于直接描绘外面的"象"，而是通过改变棱镜和滤镜的技术使用，实现表现上的突破……直到有一天这个窗口被照相机彻底堵上了，艺术家不甘心，寻找新的突围方式，玻璃的功能已经被照相机代替了，这块玻璃在空间里的意义是什么呢？有人说"我向你展示这块玻璃吧"，于是就有了现成品。到这个时候，空间里唯一的窗口已经被堵死，这个空间成为了"无"。哈罗德·泽曼在此提供了一种意识，在你的脑海里艺术又回归到了初始状态，是"无"，这个时候要做什么？

我们可以想象一下，当一个盲人进入这个"无"的空间会先做什么？如果是我，第一件事决不会是做自己真正想做的事情，而是先对这个空间进行试探性的探索，即一种勘探工作。有趣的是，展览的第一件作品是一个砸进地面的大铁球，而地面正是你进入空间后第一个接触到的元素。这个展览的很多作品都呈现出一种"刚刚迈入一个空间所做的探索性尝试"的状态，它们甚至都不怎么"艺术"。还有很多关于"测量"的作品：题目里面出现了测量，材料里出现了尺子。在测量空间之后，还有对墙面材质的置换、对边界的探索、对张力的感知、空间局限性的提示、对外部空间的想象以及对空间的直接占有。在这样一个展览里，艺术家对空间的探索愿望、掌控欲望在这些同质化的作品里体现得很强烈,这样的方法在后来的许多当代艺术作品里再次出现,因此我们会感觉到对这些方法很熟悉,甚至我在描述这些作品的时候完全不需要图片,大家就能想象得到。

当然,这个展览最关键的作用还是在于策展人让艺术家放下了自己的既定人设和路线,共同探索,开启了当代艺术的一个崭新的发展方向,向着语言更丰富、更深层、更高阶的叙事发展,阻止了现代主义时期为了打破传统艺术所采取的极端方式的过快体制化。这是我认为这个展览在策展人与艺术家两方面之所以经典、重要的原因。

我在摘要里还提到了一个问题,艺术家的身份焦虑是什么?艺术家为什么会产生身份焦虑?可能和德波顿所说的广义上的身份焦虑不完全是一码事,但有重叠的部分。比如一个在美院任教职的艺术家,当他停止艺术创作的时候,他还有一个职称,这个职称似乎在体制当中给他标定了一个技术拥有者的身份。然而对于一个职业艺术家来说,假如你没有在创作,或者你有想法但作品还没创作出来,这时候你是什么人?虽然今天有一种自由职业者,不需要上班,不需要职称,不需要体制上的认定,但他确实通过某种方法挣到了钱,这也是一种认定。艺术家的问题就在于,他既没有搞创作,也没挣着钱,这时候怎么办?其实这也是很多年轻艺术家在问我的问题,他心里会有这种关于"人设"的焦虑,关于在社会的坐标系上找到位置的焦虑。这是一种比较常规的焦虑,即德波顿所说的身份焦虑。

我觉得一个艺术家真正的焦虑不在于社会意义上的成功与否,对于当代艺术而言,当艺术家的技术优越感被取缔之后,艺术家生产的私有知识如何跟艺术史之间去寻找一个自洽的关系(即使这种自洽是带有对抗性的),或者艺术家的意愿如何跟艺术之间形成自洽,这才是对艺术家而言比较关键的问题。这个问题在策展人身上也一样。焦虑虽然在今天是一个特别烂俗的词，但它反映的本质在于你真正面对的问题在哪儿，你的焦虑才在哪儿。你找了一个虚假的学术问题，其实根本不在意、不困扰，该吃饭吃饭，该睡觉睡觉，那么这个问题并不是你焦虑的根源。

现场交流：艺术是可以穿透知识的

学员：我很好奇艺术家和策展人之间的张力，是否有时也是一种具有争夺性和竞争性的关系？如果艺术家和策展人共同呈现一个展览，在进行展览的书写时两方产生矛盾，或者策展人对于艺术家的风格、流派在艺术史上的定位与艺术家本人无法达成统一的时候，以谁的意志为优先？是艺术家说服策展人还是策展人说服艺术家？

学员：我顺着这个问题也想进一步提问孙老师，作为艺术家，当作品完成、离开创作者自身的话语体系、进入到你认可的公共展示空间中去的时候，你会以什么样的心态去看待策展人包括观众对你的作品进行的再解读或者知识再生产，尤其是当这种解读与你本身想要表达的意思可能存在较大落差的时候？

孙原：我觉得保持误解对于艺术家来说非常重要。我今天说的所有的话都有可能是错误的，对于一个学策展专业的人来说可能是非常业余的。我觉得这个错误就挺好的，艺术家和策展人之间（实际上在这里策展人就代表着一种权力），包括跟资源之间、跟观众之间，与其达成共识，不如保持误解。作为艺术家要清楚自己的人设是什么，如果你怀着一个辩手的心态想要与策展人一争高下，那你的作品应该是你的辩论。如果你是一个艺术家，那么艺术是可以穿透知识的。今天我说了这么多关于几阶知识的讨论，其实艺术家可以知道，也可以不知道。因为艺术家要足够好的话，他可以用他的方式来穿透所有的知识壁垒，这个时候，误解对他而言可能还是一种保护。当你试图去达成共识的时候，就没有欲望去穿透那个知识壁垒了，反而创作力会下降，你会缺失那些可以提供给人类的最闪光的才华。在我的底线许可的情况下，策展人用什么方式去诠释作品都行，但如果改变作品实质性的东西，我会直接拒绝。这样就比较简单，艺术家在清楚自己的人设之后，无论在世俗层面是否有足够的力量，我需要用这个人设该有的方式来应对所有问题。

■

For the two evolving concepts of "artist" and "curator", their relationship must be uncertain and fluid. With this topic here, I would like to talk about the following questions: What phases will an artist go through? How different is an artist's way of thinking from a curator when it comes to art? Where does their thinking start and what is their status anxiety? How have artists and curators today changed compared to the past? To what extent today's artists need curators? What kind of artists need what kind of curators? How would artists like curators to change? How would curators like artists to change? Or how can artists and curators work together to be more what?

Sun Yuan: Do Artists Need Curators?

Artist as an "artist": a good thing about art is that it doesn't need to be correct

Hello, everyone. I'm Sun Yuan, and my topic today is "Do artists need curators?" I see myself as an "artist". I am not an expert in philosophy, yet I think the relationship between philosophy and art may be similar to that between psychiatry and mental patients—study requires a studying object. To be honest, I feel that I am not qualified to give you a speech. Sitting here, I feel more like a research object for some of you who study art and philosophy to observe. What I am going to say is not necessarily correct, but one good thing about art is that it does not need to be correct. If you have any question or doubt about what I say, feel free to raise it. We will discuss about it and learn from each other.

In 2019, when I attended the Venice Biennale, I also went to the Academy of Fine Arts in Florence and Rome to give a lecture. I had the opportunity to talk to young Chinese students who went there to study art. Through our communication, I find that these young art students (many of whom are majored in contemporary art) are eager to understand what art is. They study at the birthplace of Western classical art. It seems they stand close to art, but they don't understand it, as if there is a thin layer of paper between them and art. Their questions are quite simple, and I sense a lack of creative thinking when they learn. In fact, studying art does not mean that the artist only starts to create when he finishes study, but that he must develop a method when he learns. This method is not necessarily correct, but it can help him. Correctness is often useless, and truth is correct nonsense. When artists produce a work, curators organize an exhibition, and scholars write an art review and do research, mostly they create a method of thinking.

I have three videos here. The first video features Peng Yu's and my work *Can't Help Myself* [Fig.1, P6&P7] at the Venice Biennale 2019. It was also on show at the Guggenheim Museum back in 2016. In fact, our initial idea was to make the robot work ceaselessly, and it would stop the liquid on the floor from spreading with the mechanical arm. At first, we did not want to have it displayed in a glass cabinet, but the robot is very powerful and fast. The art museum required that the work be isolated from people to prevent any injury when people come close to the machine. Therefore, it was all covered by glass when exhibited. It is the same as working in a transparent enclosed workshop. The liquid on the floor is a pigmented edible thickener. The basic principle of this work is similar to the scenario when water pours onto the table from a tilted bottle, you will spontaneously stop the water with your hand and temporarily keep it in a safe range from dripping onto the ground. In this work, the rotating machine has a scraper at the end of the mechanical arm and keeps working to contain the liquid around it within certain range.

This is the other work *Dear* Peng Yu's and mine showed at the Venice Biennale Fig.2, P8.

In 2013, we had a project *If Seeing Is Not an Option* Fig.3, P9 at the Pinchuk Art Center in Kiev, Ukraine. In this project, we organized a boot camp in the Art Center to train people how to use weapons. Initially we wanted to invite people from China to participate there, but encountered many difficulties in implementation. At last, we decided to recruit local volunteers in Ukraine. The locals were enthusiastic, and many people signed up. In the end, 18 volunteers passed the political background checks and participated in the boot camp. The training focused on disassembling and assembling weapons, blindfolded, under the instruction of professional army instructors. After a week of training, most participants could disassemble and assemble in about a minute. There was also a lesson every Thursday when a Ukrainian weapon expert came to teach how to use various weapons. The boot camp was meant to go on for half a year, but lasted only a few months in reality. It is not easy to realize such a project in an art museum. The organizer had to obtain an approval from the government, and built a huge cage inside the museum. For security reasons, all viewers who wanted to experience this work must have their passports checked first and finish registration. Half a year after this project, a revolution took place in

Ukraine, and the statue of Lenin in the square close to the Art Center was knocked over. The revolution took place certainly not because of us, however, after the revolution, I suddenly understood why so many locals were enthusiastic about signing up for our project— they had such a desire. I think it is interesting, because of the relation.

Artist as a "curator": unlived by what is seen.

Besides creation, I have also curated exhibitions. Five years ago, I curated an exhibition "Unlived by What is Seen" ^{Fig.4, P10&P11} in three large art spaces in Beijing, i.e. Galleria Continua, Pace Gallery, and Tang Contemporary Art. It is not an impromptu exhibition.

There are different modes of exhibitions, such as self-organized ones, propositional ones, impromptu ones, and lightweight, small-scale ones presented on public media platforms. When I was designing this exhibition, I thought about which mode to use for a long time. When I was young, I was interested in art. I would go to and participate in exhibitions. I lived in 798 Art Zone at that time, where there were many exhibitions every day and dozens of openings a week. After some time, I stopped seeing any exhibitions. For many years, young Chinese artists have been producing art that increasingly look like contemporary art——they are good at installations and decorations, using a lot of very abstract videos and ready-made items. In terms of production and quality, their works are similar to today's contemporary art. I have been thinking since then, what is the relationship between this kind of work and the artist who makes it? Suppose that there are no galleries, art museums, or contemporary art in this world, what do they do? Would they still make this ready-made thing? Would they put tables, benches, and wires in an exhibition room, and give the pile a title? Would they do that? I have serious doubts about what artists do. As artists, we create art and hold exhibitions every day without thinking about why we do it, and what we do it for. It seems that it is only because we went to art college. Also, it seems (a myth) that today's contemporary art is not contemporary enough without making ready-made items, and today's art is not artistic enough without multimedia devices. I have some doubts about this, so I talked to some artists.

There was this place called Heiqiao Art Zone where a group of artists lived. I got to know their works. Some works were not mature, but I did not look to present them as mature works. My team and I thought that we should show interesting attempts the artists made in life, and it did not have to be works. In the end, more than thirty artists/artist groups participated in the exhibition, and we recorded a video of each artist and asked them to introduce what they did. If the artist had evidence or did something, he could bring it to the exhibition. However, the exhibition is not about the documents or "works". The participating artists include Li Yongbin and Zhao Bandi. I think they share a similar state.

This exhibition received much attention at the time. Many young artists came to see it. They were affected and gave me a lot of feedback. I think the main purpose of this exhibition is to make people reflect on the purpose of art, although it seems that these young artists did not continue along this path after the exhibition and some went to make that kind of contemporary art again. I think it is a pity. However, must this form be carried on by many artists in their creation? I don't think so. An exhibition like this makes artists give up their persona and return to a basic, primitive state. Throughout the artistic career of an artist, whatever inspiration or stimulation a curator may give him, the ultimate suggestion may be not to forget the most important thing about art, rather than making him continue a certain form or method.

Artists vs. Curators

Back to the topic today, artists definitely need curators, but what should artists do together with curators? How do they cooperate? Here we are talking about curators in an academic sense, instead of those who can only find money and resources. The latter is more like film producers and what they do is mostly administrative work. After the emergence of "independent curators", how do they relate to art? What communication do artists have with such curators?

In general, I think there are two major ways for artists and curators to work together, i.e. summarization and co-production. These two working methods are equal, although some exhibitions may be accomplished through summarization or co-production, while others may be done through both, such as the ECP exhibition curated by Zhang Yingying. At the outset of a co-produced curation, the artist may have not yet produced any work or the work the curator wants. The curator will suggest a path or help the artist realize his creation. During the co-production, the less ideal way is propositional creation, while the ideal way is that the artist can withdraw from his established persona and try a new direction with the intervention of the curator.

Both as producers of knowledge, what is the difference between the artist and the curator? I think the fundamental difference lies in their positions on the ladder of knowledge: the artist at the elementary stage decides when knowledge emerges and produces private knowledge from "nihility"; the curator at the first stage does not produce private knowledge, but pays attention to the fact that the artist produces it and decides how first-stage knowledge emerges based on his access to private knowledge, so the knowledge produced by the curator is not private but shared with the artist.

An independent curator in modern times keeps up with both the artist and other people's interest in the artist. That is to say, the curator not only makes curatorial plans on the artist, but also develops a strategy in response to other curators; while positioning the artist, the curator also compares his way with other ways of positioning. This indicates that the curator has entered the second stage of knowledge production. We can see how special a curator is at this stage.

The curator at the third stage will go further and think about the historical dimension: What is the meaning of my work during the development of art history or exhibition history? Did this idea ever occur in art history? Will it have a major influence on future art phenomena or evidence? If this idea has occurred before, or it seems to have no major influence on future art landscape, will I still do it? This dimension requires the curator to think, and tests the curator's capability.

The quality of curation is not directly determined by the stages of knowledge production, be it first, second, or third. Instead, it depends on whether the knowledge produced at the stage is effective. Similarly, artists also need to know what contemporary artists are doing and consider the historical dimension, although it is not always the case and there are artists who only produce private knowledge. We are still talking about the fundamental difference between the artist and the curator. Even if both of them stands at the third stage of knowledge production, the knowledge produced by the artist is ultimately private. Then when does the artist need the curator to intervene? What kind of intervention is needed? I think we need to take it from a utilitarian perspective. Only when the curator stands at a different stage of knowledge from the artist can the curator's intervention be especially valuable.

We have noticed the curation of many solo exhibitions. If the artist is capable of good summarization, he actually does not need the curator at all. Many biennials or group exhibitions organized by official institutions simply classify works by proposition without producing any knowledge from a higher stage than the artist's creation. In this case, the curator and the artist are standing at the same stage of knowledge, so it is no different from the artist introducing himself. When the curator participates in the work of an artist, he should at least have the knowledge of stage one or two. In other words, the curator should see the artist's value, as well as what other artists are doing, and even what other curators think about the artist and what measures they have taken respectively. The curator with third-stage knowledge is like a film producer. He can remind the artist to develop or to improve the sense of questioning and strategy for expression when the artist is engrossed in producing private knowledge. He can even exert a direct influence on the artist for him to drop his established persona and try a new path.

I have put it in an abstract way, and now I'll give some concrete examples to clarify it as much as possible. Zhang Yingying's exhibition in the ECP 2019, as mentioned by Wang Luyan, is relevant to the exhibition "When Attitudes Become Forms". The exhibition curated by Harald Szeemann in 1969 is important, because it is widely recognized that Harald Szeemann established the identity and working method of "independent curators" in this exhibition. From my perspective as an artist, one of the characteristics of this exhibition is that the participating artists do not have strong individuality. The exhibition may still hold good if the name list of artists is mixed up or swapped, because none of the artists has a personal narrative.

Another characteristic is that after the exhibition, many artists did not start from there and continue their work in the same direction. For example, the well-known installation works by Claes Oldenburg in this exhibition ^{Fig.5, P18} has absolute no connection with his pop sculpture language later. Harald Szeemann called on and brought together a group of young artists who were future masters to this exhibition, through which he opposed the ossified formalism and abstract expressionism of his time. Because of him, all the artists, including those who already had a mature style such as Joseph Beuys, and others who were exploring their own path, returned to an elementary stage in this exhibition, and made a homogeneous exploration at the stage ^{Fig.6}. In order to resist rigid abstract expressionism, minimalism, and verbalized conceptual art at the time, and oppose the aggressive formalization of the hardline methods initially adopted to overthrow art forms, Harald Szeemann as the curator proposed the saying, "live in your head" through the space, Kunsthalle Bern. Beyond the physical space for display, I think Szeemann also provided the artists with a space of "nihility" as a starting point for thinking. The artists took prompt actions in response to his call. They used the least amount of the most basic materials to produce works. It is worth noting that at the same time, Fluxus began to use "fashionable" appliances such as TV sets for creation, while Harald Szeemann and the artists returned to original materials in this exhibition.

I tried to analyze the reason why the artists showed a homogenous tendency in this exhibition. Suppose that the entire art history develops in a huge enclosed space, where there is no electricity or light but only a window. In the beginning, all artists gather in front of the only window, trying to express what they have seen from the window. Then, some realize that you can see things better and draw more three-dimensionally if you clean the window. Later, some improve the sharpness and resolution of the window with optical solutions by replacing it with a lens, a wide-angle lens. Some others see more colors through the refraction of light. Over time, artists are no longer satisfied with directly depicting the "image" seen from outside, but achieve a breakthrough in presentation by altering the use of prisms and filters...Until one day this window is completely blocked by a camera. Artists are reluctant to give up and still look for a new breakthrough. As the function of the window glass has been replaced by the camera, what is the role of the glass in the enclosed space? Someone says, "I will show you this piece of glass", so for the first time we have a ready-made work. At this point, the only window in the space has been blocked, and the space becomes "nihility". Harald Szeemann creates a sense here that in your head, art has returned to its original state, which is "nihility". What do we do now?

Just imagine what will a blind person do first when entering this space of "nihility"? If it were me, the first thing I would do is definitely not something I really want to do. I would have a tentative exploration of this space, that is, some kind of prospecting. Interestingly, in the exhibition by Harald Szeemann, the first work is a big iron ball smashed into the ground, and the ground is the first element you see when you enter the space. Many of the works on show present themselves as "making exploratory attempts when just entering a space", and they are not even very "artistic". There are also many works about "measurement": measurement in the work title, and a ruler among the other materials. After measuring the space, there is replacement of wall materials, exploration of boundaries, perception of tension, hints of space limitations, imagination about external space, and immediate occupation of the space. In an exhibition like this, the artists' desire to explore and control the space is strongly reflected in these homogenized works. These methods have been used again in many contemporary art works after this exhibition. That is why we find them so familiar that there is absolute no need of any photos when I describe these works, because you can imagine how they look like.

Most importantly, in this exhibition, the curator made the artists give up their established persona and route and explore together. The exhibition has found a new direction for the development of contemporary art towards a narrative with a richer and deeper language at a higher stage, and prevented the excessively rapid institutionalization in the modern period achieved with extreme methods taken to overturn traditional art. For these reasons, I think this exhibition is classic and important from the aspect of the curator and artists.

I raised some questions in the abstract, i.e. What is

artists' status anxiety? Why do artists have status anxiety? The status anxiety here may not be exactly the same as what Alain de Botton writes about in the broad sense, but there is something in common. In the case of an artist who teaches at the Academy of Fine Arts, he has a job title when he stops creating art. This title seems to mark him as a technology owner in the institution. However, for a professional artist, if he does not create art, or if he has an idea but does not have a work, what is he? Although there are some freelancers who do not need to go to office, and do not need a job title or institutional recognition, they do need to make money in one way or the other, which is some kind of recognition. The problem for this artist is that he has made neither artworks nor money. What should he do? In fact, this is also the question many young artists have been asking me. The artist is anxious about defining his "persona" and finding himself a position in the social coordinates. This is the ordinary anxiety, which Alain de Botton calls status anxiety.

I think an artist's ultimate anxiety is not about success in the social sense. In terms of contemporary art, when the artist's technological superiority is gone, how to build a self-consistent relationship between the private knowledge produced by the artist and the history of art (even though such self-consistency is confrontational), or how to create self-consistency between the artist's will and art?

This is the critical issue for artists, which is the same for curators. Although the word anxiety has been overused, it does reflect the essence, that is, where your real problem is, where your anxiety is. You have found a false academic problem, which you don't care about. You are not bothered. You eat and sleep when it is time to. Then this problem is not the source of your anxiety.

Q&A Session: Art Can Penetrate Knowledge

Participant A: I am curious about the tension between the artist and the curator. Do they sometimes have a competitive relationship? If the artist and the curator jointly present an exhibition and there is a conflict between the two when introducing the exhibition, or a disagreement on how to position the artist's style and genre in art history between them, whose idea is going to prevail? Will the artist persuade the curator or the other way around?

Participant B: I have a further question. As an artist, how do you feel about the re-interpretation of your work or reproduction of your knowledge by the curator and audience when you finish a work and see it leave your own discourse system for the public display space approved by you, especially when there is a huge gap between such re-interpretation and your original intention?

Sun Yuan: I think it is important for artists to maintain misunderstandings. All that I have said today may be wrong, and may sound very amateurish for a person specialized in curation. I actually think such wrongness is good. Between the artist and the curator (in fact, the curator here represents a kind of power), resources, or audience, it is better to maintain misunderstandings than to reach consensus. As an artist, you need to know what your persona is. If you want to compete against the curator with the mentality of a debater, your work should be your argument. If you are an artist, your art can penetrate knowledge. I have talked a lot about knowledge stages, yet as an artist, it is not necessary to know about them, because if the artist is good enough, he can penetrate all the knowledge barriers in his way. In that case, misunderstandings may be a protection for him. When you try to reach consensus, you do not have the desire to penetrate knowledge barriers. As a result, you will lose creativity and the most brilliant talent that could have been provided to humans. The curator can interpret my work in any way, as long as it does not cross my bottom line. I will refuse anything that changes the essence of my work. That's it. When the artist is clear about his own persona, it doesn't matter if he has enough strength in the face of the external world, because he will deal with all problems according to his persona.

■

青策充电站

联合主办：上海当代艺术博物馆、复旦大学哲学学院

工作团队

上海当代艺术博物馆：张琍莉、马慧婷、徐辰斐、邱鼎、黄彦娜

复旦大学哲学学院：袁新、林晖、沈奇岚、陈佳

实录册编辑团队

主编：孙向晨、龚彦

编辑：马慧婷、蔺佳

平面设计：邵君瑜

翻译：曾晨

校对：阮汇善

ECP Charging Station Programme

Co-organizers: Power Station of Art,
School of Philosophy, Fudan University

Programme Team

Power Station of Art: Zhang Lili, Ma Huiting, Xu Chenfei,
Qiu Ding, Huang Yanna
School of Philosophy, Fudan University: Yuan Xin, Lin Hui,
Shen Qilan, Chen Jia

Editorial Team

Editor: Sun Xiangchen, Gong Yan, Ma Huiting, Lin Jia
Graphic Design: Shao Junyu
Translator: Zen Chen
Proofreader: Ruan Huishan

青策充电站
策展与艺术哲学
工作坊

实录

ECP Charging
Station
Workshop Series:
Curating and
Philosophy of Art

Record

本次讲座由复旦大学哲学学院的张双利教授以"论文化工业的意识形态功能"为题进行讲授。以霍克海默、阿多诺的《启蒙辩证法》为核心文本，讲座将分四个层次系统讲述法兰克福学派的文化工业批判理论。首先，以理性与权力之间关系为核心线索，概要介绍《启蒙辩证法》的基本结构和核心内容；其次，分生产和消费两大环节，以"风格"和"娱乐"为核心概念，具体分析内植于文化工业中的理性机制；再次，以"无思"和"强制性模仿"为核心概念，进一步说明文化工业的意识形态功能。最后，结合当前时代背景，思考法兰克福学派文化工业批判理论的现实意义。

张双利：
论文化工业的意识形态功能

《启蒙辩证法》的核心问题：理性的自我毁灭

当今的时代，右翼崛起，新法西斯主义的概念被提出，并被用来讲述2008年危机之后的当代资本主义世界。在此背景之下，《启蒙辩证法》变成人们必须重新阅读，认真对待的又一本著作。如果我们可以用新法西斯主义去界定当下的这样一个所谓在新自由主义和资本主义裹挟下危机显露的糟糕处境的话，你会发现我们可以站在今天理解《启蒙辩证法》的时代背景。它的时代背景是经由所谓的理性所主导的进步，然后堕落到了野蛮主义。用霍克海默和阿多诺的的话来说是一种新野蛮主义。这是借助理性的、文明的逐步进展，随后抵达一种新版本的野蛮主义，究其本质还是野蛮主义。所以，进步没有导致一种人性的状态，换言之进步没有导致"人"的地位的提升，进步导致的是人性的反面——野蛮主义。上一届上海双年展的主题"Proregress"（禹步）就是想要指出以进步名义出现的整个大写的历史进程，为什么它最终实际走向了其预定目标的反面。

二战以后，人类开始整装待发，重新沿着进步的方向去实现对人和人之间关系的重新安放。2008年危机之后，人类发现好像又进入了一种彻底的野蛮主义。随后，我们看到的又是右翼民粹主义的崛起，政治正确所坚守的所有文明和礼貌被彻底打翻在地。在这种情况之下，你会发现《启蒙辩证法》这本书也许和今天还是有某种内在的暗合。我想这也是为什么上届上海双年展要回到阿多诺，从而去理解处于资本主义体系边缘地带的南美社会的生态危机和社会危机。

你可以从《启蒙辩证法》中找到的核心线索是支撑着社会现实的理性。理性主义的文明凭靠的是理性，它并不是那种想象之中、和现实生活分开、观念世界里的理性，而是刚好与之相反。理性主义的文明进程凭靠这个理性，并直接将其落地为社会现实的具体理性。这是第一个非常重要的原则，我们也是基于这个原则才能够把分析的对象集中到理性本身。而《启蒙辩证法》的核心问题是理性的自我毁灭：理性文明如何走向自己的反面。究其原因，我们可以通过一个更窄的入口思考理性本身。当然思考这个理性本身的时候，不能将它脱离现实生活，抽象地看待。因为这个理性是支撑着现实生活的理性，这个理性就是现实生活当中的社会结构，也就是现实生活中的人和自然、人和人之间关系的安排。

《启蒙辩证法》这本书实际上讨论的就是理性的自我毁灭，当我们一直凭靠的理性发生了变化或是受到伤害，它带来的实际结果就是集权主义和野蛮主义。所以这是社会现实，是一种陷入了彻底错误的社会现实，为了能够对这个彻底错误的社会现实进行思考和消化，你们要将这样一个时代交给你任务进行概念化。概念化的方式是借助于理性和现实之间的关系，把它浓缩为是理性的自我毁灭。《启蒙辩证法》对理性走向自我毁灭的这个过程进行反思框架是尼采提供的，这个框架的要点是理性与权力之间的关系，即我们所凭靠着的理性，它从来都是和支撑着人与人之间的支配和被支配关系的社会统治性的权力相结合的。理性从来不可能是解除了权力绑架的理性，理性始终和权力纠缠在一起的。这其中也隐含了一种张力关系，这个张力有两个层次。其一，任何一个人群中的强权者，他若要将自己对于他人的支配性的地位稳定，那就必须借助理性。所以在这个意义之上，理性是权力的工具。其二，只要强权者借助了理性进行统治，反而就会对他设立的强权形成限定。就是一个遵从理性的统治者，他企图通过理性来维护权力，但是理性一定会限定其权力，他讲出来的道理一定同时也使得他手里的权力被限定。所以，一方面是权力使用理性，它是工具性的；另一方面理性一旦作为支撑人和人之间的关系的根据，它一定限定权力，这是人类文明的常态。这个矛盾的双向张力关系无法相互和解，必然会时常被败坏。

随后，《启蒙辩证法》在这个结构当中去讲现代启蒙，这个现代启蒙就是从文艺复兴以来的启蒙。培根认为凭靠理性所带来的知识能够彻底消解强权。因为知识就是力量，我们不再受制于外部自然对于我们的主导。此外，培根终其一生和女王所代表的贵族体制进行艰苦卓绝的斗争，虽然培根同时也希望成为女王的宠臣。但是培根所强调的是这种知识，只要它是知识，它是无法被特权和财富所垄断。

如果这种知识意味着我们可以自行安排生活并实现幸福，那么这样的一种知识也瓦解了少数垄断群体的强权和财富。所以那时的现代人坚信理性可以消解强权，并以理性驱上帝，也驱赶了上帝形象在人间的主导者——君主和贵族。所以，在人们设想之中，这样的理性一方面可以支撑人和人之间普遍平等的关系，带来了现代民主社会；另一方面可以支撑着人们和自然之间的科学进步，带来无止境的进步和物质财富的极大充盈。

但是，我们所看到的实际情况是理性恰好走向了其反面。培根所提出的这样的一个想象与人们的生活之间产生了重大的差异。

因为生活不是用理性去瓦解强权。这也产生了三层权力关系。第一层，人和自然之间的关系也因为科学进步产生了颠倒，不再是自然主导人，而是人以为自己主导着自然。第二层权力关系是人凭靠着科学技术和机器对自然的不断主导，同时也就是掌管着科学技术和机器的一部分人对服务于科学技术和机器的另一部分人的主导，这其实是人与人之间的权力关系的重新安排。第三层次，这样的一群人借助资本和技术实现了对另一群人的掌管以及对于自然的操纵，表面上看是把生活递交到了少数人的手里，让他们变成了规定生活的上帝。但实际上这也产生了一条不归路，就是这个过程本身并不能真实的掌控在这些所谓的少数的强权者的手里。所以，在整个当代资本主义社会中，每一个人都被这个所谓的没有主体的过程所掌控。你会觉得这个生活是无主体的，而这个无主体的生活掌管着每一个人。但是你又知道生活中被掌管的人又分为强权者和弱者。强权者似乎又掌管着弱者，而这种权力关系并不能够抵消"生活是无主体的"这件事，也并不能够让无主体的生活掌管现代社会当中的每一个人。理性无法帮助我们参透这三层权力关系所产生的错误生活，所以理性失去了自知。同时，因为理性实际是支撑着强权，所以它在走向反面的过程中不再具有任何思考能力。

为了解决理性的自我毁灭，我们需要一个结构进行思考，这个结构是理性和权力之间的复杂关系。然后，我们再以这个结构为参照系来讲述现代启蒙为何走向了败坏。在这个意义之上，相较于古希腊和中世纪的启蒙，现代启蒙虽然更好地解决了复杂的结构性关系，但是它使这种结构性关系出现了彻底败坏的可能。所以才会出现法西斯主义，以及现代人彻底地被整个生活所裹挟并不知生活究竟走向何种灾难的情况。《启蒙辩证法》整本书就是围绕理性的自我毁灭，让你既能理解从古希腊到中世纪再到现代这三大环节的文明进展历程，也让你理解现代的这个环节为什么会以法西斯主义收场。

理性 - 权力与文化工业的关系

法西斯主义上台后，霍克海默和阿多诺等法兰西斯学派的知识分子都流亡到了北美。他们发现北美社会和法西斯主义统治的欧洲没有实质性的差别。所以，他们通过《启蒙辩证法》的第二章《文化工业》阐释了这个情况。北美社会实际同样将理性下降为工具，少数集团使用这个工具掌握强权并进行垄断。换言之，北美社会的根本性质也是一个全面宰制的社会。在这个全面宰制的社会当中，你的生活看似由你作主，但实际上你的生活完全是被既定的社会权力事先规定。实际上你已经失去了规定自己行动的那种理性能力，强权者利用理性生产出了一系列复杂的机制，让你在毫无知觉的情况之下，安排规划你的生活。

霍克海默和阿多诺透过北美社会异常繁荣的文化工业现象，发现这一文化工业具有马克思所说的意识形态的功能，它以理性的名义让你接受当前的生活，不管这个生活是怎样的错误。而且当你接受之后，你依然认为自己的生活本身是以自由为原则的。

在霍克海默和阿多诺看来，当时很多批判理论家对这个问题没有看清楚。当时很多批判理论家会用大众文化这个概念讲述在北美正在兴起的文化工业。但是一旦被定义为大众文化便有一个非常积极的意义，因为在那之前文化只属于少数贵族，而如果将文化下降到大众水平，这便是一个朝向着平等、自由、民主的社会迈出的重要一步。而霍克海默和阿多诺却认为这个文化工业看似让你成为文化工业产品的拥有者，但实际上它是为权力服务，它是一种对大众进行宰制的工业。所以，霍克海默和阿多诺坚决反对用大众文化理论的这样一种积极的判断来去应对眼前的正在兴盛的文化工业。因为你必须能够明白正在兴起的文化工业本身所蕴含着的毁灭性趋势，你才有可能带着这样的自觉，在文化工业领域中拉开竞争者的双方并展开两者之间永恒的博弈。

"策展"是文化工业中一个非常重要环节。按照本雅明的说法，在现代机械复制技术之前，艺术品真正价值是一种崇拜的价值。但是机械复制技术诞生后，它不再是一种崇拜价值，而是一种可以被展览的价值，可以直接地让所有的公众接触，并与之发生关系的价值。如果是从这个角度来看，你要把所谓的崇拜价值转变为展览价值，显然"展览"是极其重要的。根据《启蒙辩证法》，我们需要怀揣反思对文化工业进行重构。所以策展和艺术创作的过程中也应该坚持反思。

从1874年以后，资本主义基本上彻底转型。转型之后，我们进入了有组织的资本主义，这种资本主义是少数的资本拥有者和少数的国家权力宰制者相互合作的资本主义。这种资本主义产生的原因是因为自由业主的资本主义遇到了危机，摆在危机面前只有两条路，要么是自下而上的革命，这意味着马克思的无产阶级革命，要么是自上而下的革命。自上而下的革命是什么？自上而下的革命是资本寡头和国家所谓的实际权力掌管者的合谋。霍克海默和阿多诺认为在这个社会条件之下，会出现文化统一性。就是在文化产业高度发达的情况下，虽然文化工业产品各式各样、林林总总，但它们实际上是一个东西，这个是他所强调的一个现象。

但是霍克海默和阿多诺仍然相信文化工业很重要，文化工业是工业之中的工业。因为各个工业分掌着各个不同的领域，如果这些领域的产业要正常运营，就需要有一个产业专门来加工人们对生活的理解和想象，而这个产业就是文化工业。通过加工，它让看似无法被人消化的生活变得可亲、可理解、可接受。

但是正是因为文化工业所埋藏的齐一原则，让它需要通过一套理性机制落地。所以，文化工业不是简单的艺术创造的产业，决定文化工业成败的不是我们平常所说的美学创作，而是理性，一种为强权服务的有效工具。比如本雅明用机械复制时指的是技术复制，这就强调了文化产品生产中，我们调用了其他产品的同样生产技术，所以它是一种技术理性。技术理性强调的是可以满足不同人的需要。技术之为技术在于它所提供的东西是可以满足那些无法被工艺满足的市场需要。所以供给和需求让技术理性获得了非常正面的含义。霍克海默和阿多诺认为技术理性实际上是让统治成为可能的理性。因为它虽然的确完成了复制和大规模商品生产，但是这个技术理性所指向的这个需求不是自发的，它不是来自于受众的需要，而是被文化工业产品反向制造的需要。这个需求本身是被强权操纵的需要。所以，文化工业的理性机制可以通过制造需要，再反向制造那被不断需求的产品。这样一来，虽然整个供求关系依然还在，但其意义就彻底改变了。所以，文化工业的成与败在于文化工业的从业者是否学会了这样一种理性机制的发明和运用。

我记得上海大学开办电影学院时就强调了中国电影和西方电影最大的差别，不是中国缺乏原创性内容和好演员，而是我们缺乏可以让文化工业产品成为质量上乘的文化工业产品的那一套技术理性。这套技术理性是社会功能，所以我们如果要培养这个产业的人才，就必须培养技术理性的硬核能力。然后，你才能够去阐发硬核之外的软实力，比如你怎样思考，怎么样让它不是操纵而是批判。你要能察觉这种硬核理性机制所蕴含的负面社会功能，然后你就可以使用软向操作，对于这种硬核的理性机制进行一定程度的抵制和再加工。所以，小众电影一定是在大众电影的技术充分成熟之后才产生。因为需要先有硬核机制，然后你对硬核机制本身所蕴含着的错误倾向充分自觉，才能对这样一种硬核机制进行重造。

文化工业内部的理性机制：以"风格"和"娱乐"为核心

然后我们来看，它如何分两端去分析内植于文化工业中的理性机制。首先，文化工业是生产产品的，因为文化工业声称我不是艺术，我不生产艺术品，我只生产产品，我是为艺术市场、文化产品市场服务的。怎样理解文化工业产品的生产、怎样才能够塑造出一流的文化工业产品的生产者，这是他在文章中所要解决的问题。这个时候他用的概念是"风格"，这个概念似乎可以用来讲文化工业产品，甚至有的时候也可以讲一定的建筑、艺术作品，但仅有"风格"跟哲学是对接不上的。这时我们需要引入另外一个概念才能够讲清楚生产的问题，这个概念听起来非常抽象，叫作"图式"。图式帮助我们解决"如何去消化杂多的世界"的问题。我们在接受来自于世界的、这些杂多的内容的时候，实际上我们已经在用一个统一的模式对这些杂多的内容进行预先塑形。这样一种预先塑形在康德的哲学当中就叫"图式"。我们为什么可以理解外部世界，很重要的一点是我们在看外部世界的过程当中，已经先行加入了一种形式，而这个形式来自于我们的理性认知能力。但是在我们的理性认知能力当中的这样一个形式，它似乎只是抽象的形式，它无法跟感性的杂多对接，所以中间需要一个环节，这个中间环节就是"图式"。它把齐一的形式和感性杂多相合，悄悄地埋藏在我们的感性经验当中。所以，当任何一个人睁开眼睛观察世界，只要你有正常认知能力，你都能够看清楚凳子是凳子、桌子是桌子。这样的一种能力并不是这个世界本身让我们获得的，而是在我们的认知能力当中有一种机制，这种机制可以让我们把统一对象的形式和感性杂多的内容相合，然后把它推送到我们的经验当中，这是康德的理论。康德行哥白尼的革命无非是强调对象之所以是可被认识的，是因为对象是事先被我们进行过加工的，如果它事先没有被我们行过加工，睁开眼睛只会被世界所灼伤，永远不可能看清世界的某个片断或者某个样态。

但是这个概念和文化工业产品有什么关系？在这里讲到了我们非常熟悉的肥皂剧这样一种文化工业产品的生产，为什么要调用"图式"这个概念？因为图式这个概念当中是先存在形式，然后再是它怎样去和来自于世界的内容相合，而这样一个过程在文化工业当中会放大到极致。我们现在虽然说艺术是来自于大众的，但是到了文化工业产品的时代，艺术不是来自于大众的，艺术是掌握在和大众相分离的、文化工业产品的制造者手里的。它借助于自己的形式，从生活当中去不断拣选可以和它的形式看似无矛盾地被揉和在一起的分门别类的类目。所以形式在这里变成一个公式，这个公式把所有来自于生活各方面的东西，有平庸的、高贵的、清雅的、恶俗的……把所有这些分门别类地拣选出来，然后用这一个公式悄悄地把它加工好，加工好之后，你会看到这个形式实际上在这里完成了推送内容的功能。所以，不是形式去加工内容，而是形式去推送内容。这就好像上帝从无创有一样，做文化工业产品的人实际上是用这个形式，不断地从生活当中借用一点内容，一旦被借用来之后，就变为他文化工业产品服务的内容，而这个内容实际上是他用这个形式硬生生地拣选和创造出来的，创造出来之后他就推送出去。这意味着什么？这意味着从此以后，康德所讲的问题不需要由人的脑海当中所埋藏着的某种先天机制来完成，文化工业产品就可以完成了。文化工业产品用自己的这种齐一的模式不断地去加工生活当中的内容，借用、编织之后再推送到你面前，每一个人通过不断地接触文化工业产品，接受到了在它们当中所蕴含着的齐一的形式，最终变成了你去看世界的眼光。在这里我举一个例子，我带儿子在美国的时候，他看着蓝天白云说，"妈妈今天的天空真漂亮，跟屏保一模一样！"这个时候他还小，没有任何反思能力，我想想也没有打断他，我觉得的确挺像屏保的。屏保是文化工业产品推送给他的东西，变成了孩子去理解生活的一个滤镜或镜头，当他看惯了屏保再看眼前现实世界的时候，实际上就是由屏保作为一个背后的所谓的形式，让他去观察眼前的现实生活。这个例子告诉你，你实际上是通过文化工业产品以及文化工业产品当中所埋藏着的这个齐一的公式获得了看世界的能力。你不要误以为是有了自己看世界的能力之后、站在所拥有的理性能力之上才去消化文化工业产品，而是文化工业产品本身用这样的一种公式，对你根本还无力消化的内容先行消化，然后推送给你，于是你就借助于文化工业产品不断推送给你的这个齐一的形式去理解你所接触到的所有的对象。所以，如果说工业产品是一个镜头的话，实际上你是要借助于文化工业产品的镜头才能看世界。这就是"图式"在工业产品当中是如何被落实下来的。

"图式"在文化工业产品当中落实下来，这在文化工业产品盛行的时代意味着什么？在这里要强调的是，在这个时候很多人会说文化工业产品是杂多的，是琳琅满目的，其中有一些还是恶俗的。所以艺术一旦被下放到市场，就失去了艺术的品位，就没有了能够让我们享有有机的、共同的生活的那种统一性。这时有一些保守主义和浪漫主义的人为了表达一种乡愁般的对过去的留念而提出"风格"的概念，所以"风格"的概念是在这个背景下出来的。你看到的是一个齐一的形式借助于分门别类的生产运营方式，不断地推送出琳琅满目的商品让你眼花缭乱，你实在觉得这个生活更新速度太快，毫无章法，彻底凌乱。在这种情况之下，就会有浪漫主义的、保守主义的声音出现，这种浪漫主义和保守主义的声音要求我们重返那个曾经有着完美的有机统一性的时代。在那个时代当中，它的建筑风格、艺术作品的风格，它的日常生活所有的一切都有一种非常微妙的统一性。这种统一性让我们能够识别出那个时代、认同那个时代，是这样一个概念。

然后霍克海默和阿多诺说，这个概念本身实际上让我们认识到很多东西。第一，文化工业产品在这个意义之上是对于风格的贯彻，只不过用他的话来说叫程式化的野蛮主义。当我们用风格的时候，希望过的是一种文明且体面的生活，可是文化工业产品作为对风格的贯彻，实际上表明我们跌入到彻底的野蛮。因为在人们对风格的想象当中，风格之为风格，它最终所要成就的是一种文化能力，这个文化能力可以把生活加工为与生活内在相合的形式。但你现在是用粗暴的形式进行粗暴的推演，然后用这个粗暴的公式七拼八凑，带来各种各样只有假象意义的内容，所以是一种彻底的野蛮，是对形式和内容的双重败坏。看似是有齐一性的，是对风格的贯彻，但是把风格本身所要解决的形式与内容的关系彻底败坏，然后让人彻底丧失了面对内容的能力，所以说它是一种极致的野蛮。制造文化工业产品的这些大师们，他们所干的事情就是不留痕迹地制造野蛮。那么他怎么才能够不留痕迹的制造这种野蛮呢？实际上很简单，他用自己的一种公式或者是公式一样的形式，把它和很多内容相合。他要会用行话——比如说你是做历史题材电影的，然后你是做家庭伦理片的。不管是哪个行业都有一系列的行话，行话让所谓细致具体的内容可以被调用，调用的目的只是为了让公式可以落地。这个时候如果达到大师的境界了，最高的标准就是自然主义，就是他的的确确讲出了你在生活当中每天都经历到的东西，但是你自己没有那个公式对它进行加工，于是你觉得这个电影讲述的是我们某种微妙的生活经验，或者讲述的是那个最贴近自然的自然本身等等。所以，把这样一种风格落地的过程，就是用统一的公式对实际版本的生活进行一种巧妙的复制，复制得不留痕迹，实际上它已经变成人造的，已经变成由这个统一的公式所驾驭的，但是你觉得他讲就是生活本身。这个时候就达到了文化工业产品的最高境界，而这样的一种最高境界实际上就是风格在文化工业产品当中的贯彻。

霍克海默和阿多诺要强调的第二点是，只有当风格被贯彻、达到了对于风格的彻底败坏之后，你才能够真正明白当年的那些伟大的艺术作品和风格之间的关系是怎样的。那些伟大的艺术作品，无论是印象派的还是现代主义的，似乎有它的风格、有背后的原则和根据，但《启蒙辩证法》要告诉你，任何一个伟大的艺术作品，它的内容一定是在齐一风格的要求之下，对那个齐一的风格的否定或溢出。任何一个时代都有对于艺术作品的齐一的要求，都有对于生活理解的一种齐一的要求。伟大的艺术作品不在于对齐一性的贯彻到底，而在于它恰恰能够在这个齐一性的参照之下、统摄之下去突破统摄，能够把统摄所按捺不住的表达性的内容推送出来，这才叫伟大的艺术作品。所以，风格对艺术作品来说只有否定性真理的意义。艺术作品之伟大不是因为它有风格，而是在于它能够进行对风格的否定。而这样的一种能够对风格否定的伟大的艺术作品，当然也让风格发挥了作用，这就是阿多诺所说的否定性真理。如果说艺术让真理呈现，它也是以否定的方式呈现，并不是说在哲学当中你是靠批判靠反思，一到艺术那里你就靠对真理的直接拥抱，让真理在你的艺术作品中进行直接的流淌，哪有那么简单的事。艺术作品虽然是感性的，虽然表述的是某个特定的生命经验，但是这个特定的生命经验是要被艺术形式加工的。而在艺术形式对特定的生命经验加工的过程当中，它就受到了所身处其中的社会秩序的制约，它就有一种这样社会规范性的要求。伟大的艺术作品，如果它是表达真理，不在于它对于规范的顺从，而在于它对于这样一种强制性社会规范的自觉的否定，而且是以艺术的方式。所以要特别强调，那些对既定风格进行否定的伟大的艺术作品才使得艺术作品的价值得以呈现。与之相比，我们现在所看到的文化工业产品是对这个统一公式的技术化贯彻，而且这种技术化的贯彻要追求不留痕迹，最后把人造的内容推送为来自于生活的内容，这种文化工业生产被霍克海默和阿多诺理解为是对于艺术形式的彻底败坏，因而是一种彻底的野蛮主义。这样就解决了两大问题。第一个问题，传统和现代有什么区别，所谓的传统的艺术作品和所谓的现代技术复制品之间究竟有什么区别。第二个问题，现代文化工业所制造出来的产品，它为什么既是无比的杂多又是彻底的齐一，为什么可以有林林总总的分门别类，为什么可以不断地更新迭代。另一方面它又告诉你，所有的这些更新迭代，所有的这些无止境的差异归根结底还是一个齐一性的原则。

接下来要讲娱乐，我们现在的孩子特别容易理解，因为这是一个娱乐至死的时代。在这个娱乐至死的时代里我们重新去想文化工业，文化工业就是作为娱乐的文化工业，这究竟怎么解？而且它在这当中解出了文化工业的什么独特性？为什么要讲这个问题，因为不讲这个问题的话，你不能理解为什么文化工业产品不是去满足大众的需要的，而是去满足被制造出来的大众的需要的。这不仅仅是意味着文化工业产品何以被消费，不仅仅意味着从消费的角度去讲文化工业这个独特的产业，而且它要特别去强调：怎样让文化工业产品有效实际上就意味着怎样能够让文化工业产品和人的需要相合，而这里提到的个人的需要，是由文化工业产品自己制造出来的需要。这个过程是怎么实现的？它之所以可以落地是因为文化工业产品满足了一个非常重要的条件——制造对实际生活的彻底逃离的假象。马克思在《1844年经济学哲学手稿》里提到，人在劳动的时候觉得自己活得只不过像个动物。人在不劳动的时候，彻底地从这样一种动物般的劳动境界解除的时候觉得自己活的像个人。因而只要外在的、强制的劳动一解除，人们就会像逃避瘟疫一样地逃避劳动。就像考试一考完了，学生恨不得把书扔掉烧掉，因为整个学习的过程，对他来说是一种彻底的、外在的强制。这个机制为什么会有这样一种需求？这个需求的背后是什么？文化工业产品为什么可以打中这个需求？它又为什么是一种极致的欺骗？

我们看到《启蒙辩证法》里文化工业这一章叫"作为大众欺骗的文化工业"，不是作为大众文化的文化工业。换言之，它的确触痛了你的软肋，但问题是它永远不可能解决你的软肋，它永远不可能真实地回应你的需要。这个需要为什么会有？来自哪里？你在今天是看不清楚的，虽然你读过《1844年经济学哲学手稿》。你要从传统去看，在传统社会当中，当然他讲的这个传统社会你必须想象这是贵族社会，这是一群人对另一群人行规定的社会，这是君主和贵族掌管着整个国家，因而掌管着整个国土，因而掌管着国土上所正在耕作着的农奴的社会。在这个社会当中，人群之间的分工可以有很多种讲述，比如说你可以说是思想和劳动分离，你也可以说是财产和劳动的分离。我们中国人非常熟悉的劳心者、劳力者的说法，换算成马克思主义的语言可以说它是有产者和无产者之间的分离，你可以说它是有思想和无思想之间的分离，因为劳心者他显然可以有思想，可以行规定。但是，霍克海默和阿多诺说，在所有的这些讲法的背后，要理解现代文化工业还得再加上一个讲法，他们之间的分离实际上是艺术和娱乐的分离。艺术意味着行规定的这帮少数的特权者，他们已经从外部生活的负担当中解除出来，所以他可以在这里去行以自由为原则的艺术创作，或者是他可以去欣赏以自由为原则的艺术创作所带来的伟大的艺术作品。无论是艺术家还是艺术家背后的那些保护人，基本上都是属于这样一个群体。艺术这个环节存在，一定在结构上要求另一个环节——娱乐同时存在，就是那些大量的让特权者成为特权者的、在土地上耕作着的人，这些人基本上就是背负者，就像你在《圣经》当中所读到的，因为犯下了原罪所以一生要受苦，受苦就背负着重轭，这个重轭就是劳作，你要祖祖辈辈一生一世背负着劳作的重担。这两群人是社会生活当中共生的关系，永远不可能只有艺术没有娱乐，而这样一种娱乐显然没有意义，它就是从劳动当中的逃避。你要在娱乐当中找到意义是不可能的，所以娱乐的规定性就是无意义；而艺术你可以说它的规定性是真理，它是以一种自由的方式在感性的艺术形式当中去呈现真理的，所以二者之间是对立着的两极没错。但霍克海默和阿多诺所说的是，艺术和娱乐不仅是对立的两极，而且永远共生，后者是前者的影子，只要有前者就必然有后者，更重要的是，因为它们是如此这般的结构性共生关系，所以谁也没有能力把它融合。你绝对不可能让二者之间达到和解的统一的关系。

娱乐所回应的正是人们对于劳动负担的逃避，这样一种真实的需求。现代社会最重要的一点就是人人都在劳动都在贡献，不论劳心劳力。大家作为正在贡献着的整个群体当中的个人，相互平等，应该抽象地承认每一个人都具有伟大的人格。正因为如此，这个所谓的只为少数特权者所享有的艺术，它显然也会被民主化。所以才会有文化工业，才会有文化工业产品，才会有文化工业产品把当年为少数特权者所垄断的伟大的艺术作品推送到大众的面前等等。在这种情况之下，是不是就没有了逃离的欲望呢？显然不可能，因为强制性的劳作依然在继续。为了让劳作可以被逃离，还是要让文化工业产品能够发挥当年的逃离的功能。所以在文化工业产品当中要对娱乐的要素加以借用。但你毕竟占有了整个文化领域，所以不仅要对娱乐的要素加以借用，同时还要借用一些当年的艺术领域中的要素。这个时候你就会看到文化工业产品完成了一个不可能的任务，就是它好像把艺术和娱乐两方的要素非常完美地吸收了，最后呈现出来的这个文化工业产品既可以有体面的艺术的气息，又可以拥有释放和逃离的功能。霍克海默和阿多诺在这里要通过这个概念告诉我们，第一这何以可能？第二在这背后究竟意味着什么？他们在这里通过"逃离"的概念告诉我们，这是何以可能的。道理很简单，就是要把工作和休闲的两极在彻底分离的假象之下，让这两极之间的分离已经不在。这意思是说你之所以可以有逃离的假象，你必须工作休闲两元。有了工作时间和休闲时间之分之后，休闲生活如何被填充？这里很重要的一点就是不需要你努力，所以不能让你去学绘画学声乐这一类的严肃艺术——这些都需要经历严格的辛苦的过程才能够达到以一种艺术形式来完成对于真理的呈现。那怎么样才能够让他毫不努力呢？很重要的一点是在文化工业产品当中要埋藏着同样的机制，这个机制让文化工业产品的消费者在不需要任何努力的情况之下，就可以自动地对这个机制当中所释放出来的一层又一层的刺激进行回应。这种刺激反应机制和你在生产当中的机械反应机制是一模一样的。

所以，文化工业产品不是让你进入到和工作状态不一样的另一种状态，而是让你在不工作的情况之下，实际的生命状态仍然和工作的状态一模一样。文化工业产品不能够真正使你处于彻底分心的状态，而是让你依然处于警醒的状态。比如你看一个肥皂剧会马上对它进行快速的反应，很快知道它是什么样的格局什么样的走势，即使你不看下去脑补都能补上，这叫警醒。我们现在所看的很多肥皂剧、特技电影或者动画电影，很多人说它没有完整的情节了，像是拍到这一集的时候还没想到后面十集怎么拍呢，但它的刺激反应机制是一样的，它在预设了你的一个反应之后再对于可以导致你的反应的这些素材进行推送。小孩为什么看"米老鼠和唐老鸭"看得那么高兴？第一因为他可以预见情节，他看到唐老鸭是笨笨的鸭子，就知道它马上要被捉弄的，而他预见到的这个捉弄很快就会以实际的画面形象推送到孩子面前。第二点很重要，为什么现代人一定要看娱乐片搞笑片？因为生活当中你少有强者的姿态，但是看搞笑片的话你永远是站在强者的姿态观看看统一的残酷的强制性的力量如何降临在剧情当中，并将各种各样的捉弄不断地施加在恶作剧对象身上。这个时候你可以跟着它的节奏不断地反应，反应过程当中又可以觉得自己没在劳作，同时还可以把自己提升到在生活当中根本没法提升的状态，即强者的姿态，然后就会感觉到一种全身心的释放。因为这种刺激反应机制不需要你主观努力它就可以调用的，而调用的过程对你来说是一种抒发，这就是逃离。这种逃离最大的"好处"是，看似你在休闲的状态中逃离了工作的负担，但是这样的一种逃离让你可以尽快适应下一步的工作负担。所以你看搞笑片很舒服，看完之后放松睡觉第二天照样满血复活去工作。如果让你看一个非常沉重的严肃电影，当中好像挖掘出了人性的某种难以言说的、复杂的、难解的东西，然后又留了一个开放的问题让你纠缠，这样第二天怎么进入工作状态？怎么能够顺理成章地重新按照这个刺激反应的方式去安排自己的日常生活？所以这种休闲娱乐也是一种"充电"，它让你更好地返回到有着固定的工作机制的生活当中去。

在这里面要强调的是，这种逃离具有非常强烈的欺骗性质，因为它是通过制造欲望来压抑你的欲望，又通过压抑你的欲望，制造出对你新的产品的欲望。这样一来，整个文化工业产品不是对需求的满足，而是对欲望的压抑和对需求的不断制造。这种对欲望的压抑和对需求的不断制造使得文化工业产品可以长流水不断线，即是它永恒地需要翻新，它不断地需要续集，但任何一个更新都不会满足你的欲望，都不会使你的需求得到真实的实现。这里举了一个例子说明文化工业产品为什么是欺骗性的，虽然我觉得这个例子放到当代世界不是很成立。假如想象文化工业已经彻底破产，例如所有的电影院都关门了，这个时候最受到真实伤害的人在他那个年代只有两类人：第一类是家庭主妇，第二类是流浪汉。家庭主妇没有工作和休闲的两元，因为永远在家庭当中，看似根本就不工作但是永远在工作。在这个情况之下，电影院的电影对她来说没有意义，她不需要对于电影进行自动反应等等，她可能还没有这个能力，但是电影院本身灯光一熄，荧幕一上演，这个东西就使得她进入了和生活不一样的又一个境界。所以电影院这个空间的存在，实实在在为家庭主妇们拉开了一个和工作不一样的休闲世界，这个休闲的世界和工作之间唯一的差别在于断裂。所以如果把电影院关了，家庭主妇肯定是真正的受害者。而平常经常去电影院享受休闲时光的人，电影院关了对他们来说没有真实的伤害，因为电影本身对他来说也没有真实的帮助。另一类是流浪汉，他们来电影院是为了找到一个遮风躲雨的避难所，因此电影院的关闭对他们而言也是实际的生活损失。他们用这个两个反例去证明文化工业产品好像只具有欺骗的性质。但是，现代人会觉得离开了文化工业产品我就活不下去。这就意味着这个刺激反应机制不仅需要在工作当中被不断地实现，也需要不断地被隐藏被遮蔽，让人依然身处刺激反应之中又觉得没有在劳作。这样的一种欺骗式的环节，对于文化工业产品充斥之后的年代里长大的人来说也变成了一个必要的东西。但是在霍克海默和阿多诺那个年代还没有到这个程度，所以他们说文化工业产品只是一种欺骗，当看到人们对于文化工业产品的狂热，他们只是说这个狂热本身不是为了什么真的东西，实际上是一场虚幻的体验。但是到了今天，虚幻的体验已经变成必需品，这一点可能是他们当年没有想到的。

这是他们所讲的娱乐，而这种娱乐意味着对于艺术和娱乐的双重败坏。因为这个娱乐是事先安排好的娱乐、是理智化了的娱乐，这就像我们刚才说所谓的风格它是一个程式化的野蛮主义。这个娱乐作为一个事先计算的效果，先行地埋藏在文化工业产品当中。我始终记得一个例子：好莱坞拍过一个电影，专门讲一个喜剧电影导演是如何拍摄喜剧的。一部真正耗费了心血去拍摄的喜剧作品，对他来说就是一场非常明确的、把握住节奏的表演。他在大屏幕的背后去体会观众对于电影的感受，就像一个指挥家一样，准确地知道哪里会有尖叫，哪里会有大笑，他预期的所有这些尖叫大笑没有任何差错地，在恰当的时间、恰当的节奏上爆发出来，就说明这部电影成功了。这就告诉我们，所有的娱乐是由理性机制精心推送的结果。没有理性，想要拍好一个所谓的娱乐片、惊悚片不是那么容易的。怎样推送刺激、怎样预见反应、预见反应之外怎样安排整个刺激推送的节奏……这些都是非常高度浓缩的计算理性，根本不是艺术创作。而这个高度浓缩的计算理性是这里所说的娱乐被败坏的重要原因。也就是说，你作为受众早已被算计好了。就像生产线上的工人早已被机器规定好了一样，作为荧幕前的观赏者，实际上你也已经被荧幕当中所推送的信息事先规定好了。在这个意义上你是个纯粹的客体。这就是霍克海默和阿多诺对于文化工业的呈现。

■

相关阅读：
马克斯·霍克海默，西奥多·阿道尔诺：《启蒙辩证法：哲学断片》（上海人民出版社）中文版第107—152页。或是英文版 Dialectic of Enlightenment: Philosophical Fragments, Max Horkheimer/Theodor W. Adorno（Stanford University Press），第94—137页。

In this lecture, Prof. Zhang Shuangli of the School of Philosophy, Fudan University will give a speech entitled "On the Ideological Function of the Culture Industry". Based on Max Horkheimer and Theodor Adorno's *Dialectic of Enlightenment*, this lecture would give us a systematic analysis of the Frankfurt School's critical theory of culture industry. The lecture would be developed at four levels: Firstly, it would give a brief introduction to the basic structure and main points of *Dialectic of Enlightenment*, taking the relationship between reason and power as the key thread of the whole book; Secondly, it would go directly into the analysis of culture industry, taking production and consumption of cultural commodities as its two main moments. Focusing on the two key concepts of "style" and "entertainment", it then would provide a concrete analysis of the mechanism of rationality within cultural industry; Thirdly, it would go further into the explication of the ideological function of culture industry, focusing on the two key concepts of "no-thinking" and "compulsive imitation". Fourthly, it would try to provide some ideas about the relevance of Frankfurt School's critical theory of cultural industry in the contemporary context.

Zhang Shuangli: On the Ideological Function of the Culture Industry

Core Issue of *Dialectic of Enlightenment*: Self-Destruction of Reason

Today, with the rise of right-wing populists, the term neo-fascism has been proposed to describe the modern capitalist world after the 2008 crisis. In this context, *Dialectic of Enlightenment* became another masterpiece that people must read again and take seriously. If we use neo-fascism to define the dire situation in the aftermath of the crisis under neoliberalism and capitalism, you will see that we can understand the background of the time when *Dialectic of Enlightenment* was written from today's perspective. At that time, progress led by the so-called reason had descended into barbarism. In the words of Horkheimer and Adorno, it was an age of neo-barbarism. It was a new version of barbarism reached through the gradual progress of reason and civilization, which, in essence, is still barbarism. Therefore, progress did not lead to a state of humanity. In other words, progress did not lead to a higher status of "human", but to the opposite of humanity—barbarism. The last Shanghai Biennale under the title of "Proregress" intends to point out why the historical course in the name of progress finally shifted to the opposite of its intended goal.

After World War II, we began to re-establish the relationship between people along the progressive direction. After the 2008 crisis, we discovered that we may have entered a complete barbarism again. Then we have seen the rise of right-wing populism, and that all civilities upheld by political correctness have been completely overthrown. Under these circumstances, you will find that the book *Dialectic of Enlightenment* may still have some inherent coincidence with the world today. I think this is why the last Shanghai Biennale returns to Adorno to understand the ecological and social crises in the South American societies, which are in the periphery of the capitalist system.

The core clue that you can find in *Dialectic of Enlightenment* is the reason that supports social reality. A rationalist civilization relies on reason. This reason is not imaginary, separate from reality or existing in the conceptual world, but just the opposite. The rationalist civilization relies on this reason and directly implements it as the reason of social reality. This is the first important principle, and it allows us to concentrate the objects of analysis on the reason per se. The core issue of *Dialectic of Enlightenment* is the self-destruction of reason: how the rationalist civilization goes its opposite. When looking for the answer, we can think about reason in a narrower sense. Certainly, when we do it, we cannot separate the reason from real life and view it as an abstract concept, because it supports real life, and is the social structure in real life, that is, the arrangement of the relationship between man and nature, and between people in real life.

The self-destruction of reason is the exact topic discussed in *Dialectic of Enlightenment*. When the reason we have been relying on is changed or damaged, we will end up in totalitarianism and barbarism. This is the social reality, one that is completely wrong. In order to be able to think about and take in this completely erroneous social reality, you must be able to conceptualize it. During the process of conceptualization, you compress the task into the self-destruction of reason based on the relationship between reason and reality. The framework of reflection on the process from reason towards self-destruction mentioned in *Dialectic of Enlightenment* is created by Nietzsche. The main point of this framework is the relationship between reason and power, that is, the reason we rely on. Reason always combines with the power of social dominance that sustains the dominating/dominated relationship between people. Reason can never lift the abduction by power, yet instead, it is always entangled with power. It implies a tension at two levels. First, if the stronger in any group wants to stabilize his dominating position over others, he must resort to reason. In this sense, reason is a tool of power. Second, as long as the stronger relies on reason to rule, he will restrict the power he has established. That is to say, when a rational ruler attempts to maintain power through reason, reason will definitely restrict his power, and the reason he tells will also definitely restrict the power in his hands. Therefore, on the one hand, when used by power, reason is instrumental; on the other hand, once used as the basis for sustaining the relationship between people, reason will restrict power for sure. It is the normality of human civilization. This contradictory biaxial tension cannot reconcile and will inevitably corrupt from time to time.

Subsequently, *Dialectic of Enlightenment* talks about modern enlightenment under this framework, which is the enlightenment since the Renaissance. Francis Bacon believes that the knowledge brought by reason can completely eliminate power. Knowledge is power, so we are no longer subject to the external domination by nature. In addition, Bacon arduously struggled with the noble system represented by the Queen throughout his life, although he also wanted to become a favorite of the Queen. The knowledge he emphasizes cannot be monopolized by the privileged or the wealthy as long as it is knowledge.

If this knowledge allows us to arrange our own lives and obtain happiness, it also disintegrates the power and wealth of a small group of monopolies. Therefore, modern people at that time firmly believed that reason could eliminate power, and with reason, they drove away God as well as those who dominated the people in the image of God in the human world–monarchs and nobility. Therefore, in people's imagination, on the one hand, this reason can support the universal equality between people and bring about a modern democratic society; on the other hand, it can support the scientific progress between people and nature, and bring continuous progress and abundant material wealth.

However, the reality we see is that reason went to its opposite. There is a significant difference between Bacon's assumption and people's lives, because life is not about disintegrating power with reason. This also creates power relations at three levels. At the first level, the relation between man and nature has been reversed because of scientific progress. Nature no longer dominates people, and instead people think that they dominate nature. At the second level, people rely on science and technology and machines to continue to dominate nature. As a result, those who control science and technology and machines dominate those who serve science and technology and machines, which rearranges the power relation among people. At the third level, a group of people gain control of the other group of people and nature via capital and technology. It may seem that life is in the hands of a few people, making them the gods who rule life. However, in fact, this also leads to a path of no return, that is, the process itself cannot be truly controlled by these few powerful people. Therefore, throughout the contemporary capitalist society, everyone is controlled by this process without subject. You may think that life has no subject, yet the subject-free life controls everyone. You also know that those who are controlled by life are divided into the powerful and the weak. The powerful seem to be in charge of the weak, and this power relation can't offset the reality that "life has no subject", nor can it enable the subject-free life to control everyone in modern society. Reason can't help us fully understand the wrong life caused by these three power relations, so reason loses its self-knowledge. At the same time, because reason supports power, it has lost the ability to think in the process of going to the opposite.

In order to resolve the self-destruction of reason, we need a thinking structure about the complex relationship between reason and power. Then, we can use this structure as a frame of reference to tell why modern enlightenment has gone corrupt. In this sense, when compared with the enlightenment of ancient Greece and the Middle Ages, although modern enlightenment has better solved the complicated structural relationship, it has also made it possible for this structural relationship to be totally destructed. That's why fascism occurred, and modern people were so coerced by life that they did not know what kind of disastrous situation life was heading to. Focusing on the self-destruction of reason, the book helps you understand the progress of civilization in the three major moments from ancient Greece to the Middle Ages to modern times, and why the moment of modern times ended up in fascism.

Relationship Between Reason-Power and Culture Industry

After fascism came to power, intellectuals of the Franciscan school, such as Horkheimer and Adorno, were exiled to North America. They found that there was no substantial difference between North American society and fascist Europe. Therefore, they explained the situation in the second chapter of *Dialectic of Enlightenment*, "Culture Industry". North American society reduced reason into a tool, and a few groups used this tool to control power and monopolize. In other words, the fundamental nature of North American society is also an administered society, where your life seems to be determined by you, but in fact is completely prescribed by the established social power in advance. In fact, you have lost the ability of reason to determine your own actions. The powerful use reason to produce a series of complex mechanisms in order to arrange your life without you knowing it.

Beyond the phenomenon of the extremely prosperous culture industry in North American society, Horkheimer and Adorno discovered that the culture industry has the functions of ideology, in the sense of Karx Marx. It makes you accept your current life in the name of reason, no matter how erroneous this life is, and when you accept it, you still think that your life is based on freedom.

According to Horkheimer and Adorno, many critical theorists did not see this question clearly at that time, because they used the concept of Mass Culture to describe the culture industry that was emerging in North America. However, once defined as Mass Culture, the culture industry has a very positive meaning, because culture had been exclusive to a few nobles, and if culture descended to the level of the public, it was a major step towards an egalitarian, free and democratic society. However, Horkheimer and Adorno think that the culture industry seemingly makes you the owner of its products, but in fact it is an industry that serves power and administers the public. Therefore, Horkheimer and Adorno strongly oppose using such a positive judgment as the Mass Culture theory to deal with the flourishing culture industry. You have to understand the devastating trends inherent in the emerging culture industry, and then it is possible for you to pull apart competitors in the field of culture industry and start an eternal game between the two with this consciousness.

"Curating" is a very important moment in the culture industry. According to Walter Benjamin, before the modern mechanical replication technology, the true value of artwork was a value of cult. But after the birth of mechanical replication technology, it is no longer a value of cult, but a value of exhibition, that can build a direct contact and relationship with the public. From this perspective, you have to transform a value of cult into a value of exhibition, and obviously, "exhibition" is extremely important. According to *Dialectic of Enlightenment*, we need to reconstruct the culture industry through reflection. Therefore, we should also insist on the importance of reflection in the process of curation and artistic creation.

Since 1874, capitalism has largely undergone a complete transformation. After the transformation, we

entered organized capitalism, in which a small number
of capital oligarchs and state power rulers cooperate
with each other. The rise of organized capitalism is a
result of the crisis encountered by capitalism of free
enterpreneurs. There are only two ways to cope with
the crisis, either a bottom-up revolution, which means
Marx's proletarian revolution, or a top-down revolution.
What is a top-down revolution? It is a conspiracy of
capital oligarchs and the ones who hold real power
in the country. Horkheimer and Adorno believe that
cultural unity will emerge under such social condition,
that is, when the culture industry is highly developed,
no matter how various and numerous products of the
culture industry are, they are one thing in essence.
This is a phenomenon they underline.

Nevertheless, Horkheimer and Adorno still believe that
the culture industry is important and it is an industry
among industries. Each industry is in control of a
different field, and for the industries in these fields
to operate normally, it requires a specific industry
dedicated to processing people's understanding and
imagination of life, which is the culture industry.
Through processing, the culture industry makes the
seemingly indigestible life accessible, understandable,
and acceptable.

However, precisely because of the principle of
sameness embedded in the culture industry, it needs
to be implemented through the system of rational
mechanism. Therefore, the culture industry is not
simply an industry of art creation. It is not what

we usually call aesthetic creation that determines
the success or failure of the culture industry, but
rationality, an effective tool for power. For example,
when Walter Benjamin talks about mechanical
reproduction, he refers to technical reproduction and
emphasizes that we transfer the same production
technology of other products to the production of
cultural products, so it is a technical rationality. The
technical rationality emphasizes that it can meet
the needs of different people. Technology is the way
it is, because what it makes can meet the market
needs that cannot be met by handcrafts. Therefore,
the relationship of supply and demand give technical
reason a very positive meaning. Horkheimer and
Adorno believe that the technical rationality is actually
the rationality of domination. Although the technical
rationality has completed replication and large-scale
production of goods, the demand it points out is not
spontaneous, because it is not from the audience's
need, but from the need to be reversely manufactured
by products of the culture industry, which is a
manipulated need. Therefore, the rational mechanism
of the culture industry can reversely manufacture
products that are in constant demand through
producing needs. In this way, although the whole
supply-demand relationship still exists, its meaning has
completely changed. Therefore, the success or failure
of the culture industry depends on whether the culture
industry practitioners have learned the invention and
application of such a rational mechanism.

I remember when Shanghai University set up Shanghai

Film Academy, it emphasized the crucial difference between Chinese and Western movies. It is not that China lacks original content and good actors, but that we lack the technical rationality that is key for producing quality products in the culture industry. This technical rationality has important social function, so if we want to train talent in this industry, we must first cultivate the hardcore ability of the technical rationality, and then we can develop the soft power beyond the hard core, such as how we think and how to criticize not to manipulate. We need to be able to perceive the negative social functions contained in this hard-core rational mechanism, so that we can use soft operations to resist and reprocess this hard-core rational mechanism to a certain extent. Therefore, cult movies can only be produced when the technology of mass movies is fully mature, because it is necessary to first have a hard-core mechanism, in order to fully recognize the tendency of wrong development in the hard-core mechanism and then to reconstruct the hard-core mechanism.

Rational Mechanism Within the Culture Industry: With "Style" and "Entertainment" as the Core

Next, let's look at how it analyzes the rational mechanism embedded in the culture industry at both ends. First of all, the culture industry produces products. It claims that it is not art, and does not produce works of art but products, and that it serves the art market and the cultural product market. How to understand the production of products in the culture industry and how to create a first-class producer of such products are addressed by Horkheimer and Adorno in this chapter on culture industry. The concept he uses here is "style", which seems applicable to culture industry products and even to architectural and artistic works in some cases. But for the philosophical analysis of the rational mechanism within culture industry, only this concept of style is not enough. Therefore, we need to introduce another concept to clearly address the question about production. This concept is called "schema". Schema helps us to solve the question of "how to digest the manifold (*mannigfaltige*) world". When we take the manifold content from the external world, we are actually pre-shaping the manifold content with a homogenous pattern, and such pre-shaping is called "schema" in Kantianism. Why can we understand the external world? One key reason is that we employ a form before we look at the external world, which comes from "understanding" (our rational cognitive ability). However, this form is only an abstract form of our rational cognitive ability, and cannot be connected with perceptual manifold (*mannigfaltigkeit*), so an intermediate link is necessary, i.e. "schema". It connects the homogenous form with perceptual manifold, and stealthily hides it in our perceptual experience. Therefore, when anyone opens his eyes to the world, as long as he has normal cognitive ability, he can clearly see that a stool is a stool and a table is a table. Such capability is not bestowed by the world itself, but a mechanism in our cognitive ability. With this mechanism, we can combine the form of a unified object with the content of perceptual manifold, and then introduce it into our experience. This is the Kantian theory. Kant's "Copernican Revolution" emphasizes that an object is recognizable, because it is processed by us in advance. If not so, our eyes would be overwhelmed by the external world when we open them, and we would never really realize a segment or state of the world.

Yet what does this concept have to do with culture industry products? When we talk about the production of culture industry products such as soap operas that we are very familiar with, why do we use the concept of "schema"? Because schema first exists in the form, before integrating with the content from the world, and such process will be amplified to the extreme in the culture industry. Although we now say that art comes from the mass, it was not so in the era of culture industry products. Back then, art was not from the mass, but in the hands of producers of culture industry products that were separate from the mass. With its own form, schema constantly chooses from life the categories that can be kneaded with its form in a seemingly un-contradictory way. In this way, the form becomes a formula, which categorizes everything from all aspects of life, mediocre, noble, elegant, and vulgar...and stealthily processes it. Afterwards, you will see that the form actually plays the role of feeding the content. Therefore, the form does not process the content but feed it. Like God created everything out of nothing, those who make products of the culture industry constantly use the form to borrow content from life. Once borrowed, it becomes the content of the products and services of the culture industry. This content of the culture industry is forcibly picked and created by the product maker in this form, and then fed after creation. What does it mean? It means that ever since then, there is no need to turn to some innate mechanism hidden deep in the human mind to resolve the questions proposed by Kant, because culture industry products themselves can answer the questions. Culture industry products use this homogeneous model to continuously borrow, fabricate, and process the content in life, and then feed it to people. Through continuous contact with culture industry products, everyone receives the homogeneous form contained in the products, which eventually changes his view of the world. I'll give you an example here. When I was in the United States with my son, he looked at the blue sky and white clouds and said, "Mama, the sky is so beautiful today, exactly the same as the screensaver!" He was then still very young and was not yet mature enough to be self-reflective. So, I did not interrupt him. But I knew clearly that screensaver was something culture industry products fed to him, and it became a filter or lens for him to understand life. When he looked at the real world in front of him after being used to the screensaver, the world was in fact a form behind the screensaver. Let him observe the real life in front of him! This example tells you that you actually gain the ability to see the world through culture industry products and the homogeneous formula embedded in culture industry products. Don't be mistaken that you take in culture industry products only when you have the ability to see the world and stand on the basis of your rational ability, but culture industry products per se use such a formula to digest something you are still unable to digest and then feed it to you. As a result, you use the homogeneous form that culture industry products keep feeding to you to understand all the objects you come into contact with. Therefore, if culture industry products are a lens, you have to rely on it to see the world. This is how the "schema" is implemented in culture industry products.

What does it mean in the heyday of culture industry products when "Schema" is implemented in culture industry products? It should be emphasized here that at this time, many people would say that culture industry products are manifold, and some of them are vulgar. Once art is descended to the market, it will lose its artistic taste and there will be no such unity that allows us to enjoy an organic common life. Therefore, some conservative and romantic people put forward the concept of "style" to express a nostalgic memory of the past. This is how the concept of "style" came about in this context. What you see is a homogeneous form based on categorized production and operation methods, constantly feeding a dazzling array of commodities. You just feel that this life updates too fast, and appears unruly and completely messy. Under such circumstances, there comes a voice of romanticism and conservatism, asking us to return to the era that once had perfect, organic unity. In that era, the style of architecture, artworks, and everything in its daily life had a very delicate unity, which allows us to identify that era and identify with that era. This is the concept of "style".

According to Horkheimer and Adorno, the concept itself actually makes us recognize many things. First, culture industry products in this sense are the implementation of style, or in their words, "stylized barbarism". We hope to live a civilized and decent life when we use style, but the implementation of style in culture industry products proves to us that we have plunged into a complete barbarism. In people's imagination, style is what it is, because it is meant to ultimately develops a cultural ability, which can process life into a form that is intrinsically compatible with content. However, in the production of cultural industry products, only a rough form is used to make a rough deduction, and then a rough formula is used to put together a variety of content that has nothing but the illusionary meaning. Therefore, it is a complete barbarism, the simultaneous destruction of both form and content. It seems to be homogeneous, and consistent in style, but the relationship between the form and the content to be solved by style is completely corrupted, and people completely lose the ability to face the content. Therefore, it is an extreme barbarism. Masters of culture industry products simply produce barbarism without leaving any traces. How can they do so? It is actually very simple. They combine their own formula or a formula-like form with many contents. They must be able to use jargon, e.g. you make historical movies, and you make family ethics television series. Every industry has its own jargon, that allows the detailed and specific content to be transferred. The only purpose of content transfer is to implement the formula. At this point, if he is a master, the highest standard is naturalism, that is, he tells about your daily experience in life. Since you yourself don't have the formula to process it, you think the movie is about your subtle life experience, or about the nature itself that is closest to nature, and so on. Therefore, the implementation of such a style is about making an ingenious copy of the actual version of life without any traces via with a unified formula. Life has become manmade and controlled by the formula, but you still think he is talking about life itself. This is the highest level of culture industry products, and it is actually the thorough implementation of style in culture industry products.

The second point that Horkheimer and Adorno emphasize is that only after the style has been implemented and completely corrupted, can you truly understand the relationship between those great works of art and style. Great works of art, be it impressionist or modernist, seem to have their style, principles and foundations behind them, but *Dialectic of Enlightenment* wants to tell you that for any great work of art, its content must be the negation or overflow of the same style as it is at the same time meeting the requirement of such a style. In any era, there is a unified requirement for artworks and for the understanding of life. A great work of art is not about the thorough implementation of unification, but that it can break through it with the reference of it and express the content that cannot be held back by it. This is what we call a great artwork. Therefore, for an artwork, style only carries the meaning of negative truth. The greatness of an artwork is not because it has style, but because it can negate style. A great artwork that can negate style can also let style play a role. This is what Adorno calls "negative truth". If art tells truth, it tells it in a negative way. It is not to say that one criticizes and reflects in philosophy, but directly embraces truth in art and let truth directly flow in the artwork. It would never be this simple. Although artworks are perceptual and expressive of a specific life experience, this specific life experience is processed by the forms of art and restricted by the social order in which it is located when being processed. It is a social normative requirement. For a great work of art, if it expresses truth, it is not about its normative obedience, but its conscious denial of such a mandatory social norm, in an artistic way. Therefore, it should be emphasized that only the great artworks that negate the established style show the value of artworks. In contrast, culture industry products we are seeing nowadays are the traceless technical implementation of the unified formula. They finally feed the artificial content as the content from life. Horkheimer and Adorno see it as a complete corruption of the forms of art, and therefore, a complete barbarism. In this way, two major problems are solved. The first question is, what is the difference between tradition and modernity, and what is the difference between so-called traditional works of art and products of modern technical reproduction?

The second question is, why products of the modern culture industry are both incomparably multifold and completely homogeneous? Why are there so many different categories, and why can they be continuously iterated, although on the other hand, it tells you that all these iterations and endless differences are ultimately a principle of homogeneity?

Next, I'm going on to talk about entertainment. Today's children are particularly easy to understand, because this is an age of amusing ourselves to death. In this particular era, we rethink the culture industry as entertainment. What does it mean? What is the uniqueness of culture industry in this regard? Why am I talking about this issue? Because if one does not talk about it, one can't understand why culture industry products are not made to meet the needs of the public, but to meet the artificially created needs of the public. It takes more than the understanding of how culture industry products are consumed and the introduction of the uniqueness of culture industry from the perspective of consumption, but also the special attention to how to make culture industry products effective, which means how to match culture industry products up with people's needs. The needs mentioned here are the ones created by culture industry products. How to match the two up? They can be matched up, because culture industry products meet a crucial requirement–to produce the semblance of a complete escape from real life. Marx explains in 1844 Economic and Philosophical Manuscripts that people at work feel that they live like animals, yet when they are not working and completely lifted from this animal-like working state, they feel that they live like humans. Therefore, once the external and compulsory labor were lifted, people would evade labor as if it was a plague. Just like when an exam is over, students would like to throw away and burn their books, because the entire learning process is a complete external coercion for them. Why is there such a need in this mechanism? What is behind this need? Why can culture industry products meet this need? Why is it actually only an extreme deception?

We can see that the chapter about the culture industry in *Dialectic of Enlightenment* is entitled "The Culture Industry: Enlightenment as Mass Deception", instead of as mass culture. In other words, the culture industry does refer to people's real concern, but the problem is that it will never tackle their problems or truly respond to their need. Why is there such a need? Where does it come from? You can't have a clear idea from today's perspective, even if you have read 1844 Economic and Philosophical Manuscripts. You have to look at the traditional society. In the traditional society, which, of course, you must picture as an aristocratic society, a group of people make rules for the other group of people. Monarchs and nobility are in charge of the entire country, the entire territory, and every serf who are farming on the territory. In this society, the division of labor among the crowd can be described in many ways, e.g. the separation of thought and labor, and the separation of property and labor. We Chinese are familiar with the notion of mental laborers and manual laborers, which in the words of Marxism is people with property and people without property. You can say that it is the separation between thought and no-thought, because mental laborers can obviously have thoughts and make rules. However, Horkheimer and Adorno say that behind all these notions, we need another notion to understand the modern culture industry, that is, the separation of art and entertainment. Art means that a few privileged people who make rules have been relieved from the burden of external life, so that they can create art or appreciate great works of art produced under the condition of freedom. Largely, artists and patronages behind the artists all belong to this group. The existence of the moment of art structurally requires the concurrent existence of another moment– entertainment. That is, there must be another group of people, who make the privileged become privileged. The ones farming on the land basically become the bearers. Their living condition is just like that described in *Bible*: you commit the original sin, so you have to suffer all your life. When you suffer, you bear the grievous yoke, i.e. working. You need to bear the heavy burden of working generations after generation forever. Horkheimer and Adorno point out that these two groups of people have a symbiotic relationship in social life. There can never be only art without entertainment, yet such entertainment is obviously meaningless and is an escape from labor. It is impossible to find meaning in entertainment, so the determinant of entertainment is meaninglessness. In contrast, you can say that the determinant of art is truth, and art presents truth in a perceptual form of art in a free manner. Therefore, it is true that art and entertainment are opposite poles. However, according to Horkheimer and Adorno, art and entertainment are not only opposite poles, but also permanent symbiosis. The latter is the shadow of the former. As long as the former exists, the latter must exist, and more importantly, they are so structurally symbiotic that no one has the ability to integrate them. No one can ever reconcile or unify the two.

Entertainment exactly responds to people's real need to escape the burden of labor. But people would say that the most important point about modern society is that everyone is working and contributing, mentally or manually. Everyone is equal as an individual that is contributing in the entire group, and it should be abstractly recognized that everyone has a great personality. Because of this, art that is exclusive to a few privileged people can be democratized; the culture industry as well as culture industry products come along; culture industry products can feed to the public the great works of art that were monopolized by a few privileged people, and so on. Under such circumstances, is there no desire to escape? It is clearly impossible, because mandatory labor persists. In order to make labor escapable, it is necessary to let culture industry products play their role of escape. Therefore, culture industry products borrow the elements of entertainment. Moreover, since culture industry products take up the entire cultural field, so they borrow not only the elements of entertainment, but also some elements from the art field. At this point, you can see that culture industry products have completed an impossible task. It seems that after perfectly taking in the elements of art and entertainment, they can have both a decent, artistic quality and the function of a release and escape. Here Horkheimer and Adorno use this concept to explain: first, how is this possible? Second, what does it mean behind it? They use the concept "escape" to tell us how it is ever possible. It is very simple: you firstly produce the semblance of the total separation between work and leisure as two opposite poles, then you actually make the real difference between these two spheres non-existent. This means that you must have the separation between work and leisure in order to have the illusion of escape. With the difference between working time and leisure time, how can leisure life be filled in? It is important that you don't work hard in your leisure time, so you can't learn serious art such as painting and vocal music, because you need to go through a rigorous and arduous process to be able to present truth in such an art form. What can you make no effort? It is important that the same mechanism is hidden in culture industry products, which allows consumers of culture industry products to automatically react to stimuli released by the mechanism on various layers without making any effort. The stimulation and reaction mechanism is exactly the same as the mechanical reaction in production.

Therefore, culture industry products are not meant to put you in another state different from the working state, but make your actual state of life exactly the same as your working state when you are not working.

Culture industry products can't really completely distract you, but can keep you being alert. For example, when you watch a soap opera, you will quickly react to it and soon understand its structure and plot. Even if you don't finish it, you know what is going to happen based on your assumption. This is called being alert. In the case of a lot of today's soap operas, stunt movies, or animated movies, many people complain that there is no plot, and it seems those who made them didn't think about the next ten episodes when filming this one. Even so, the stimulation and reaction mechanism is the same, because it presets one of your reactions and feeds the materials that can generate your reaction. Why do children enjoy "Mickey Mouse and Donald Duck" so much? First, because they can foresee the plot. They know that Donald Duck is a stupid duck and is about to be tricked, and the trick they foresee is soon fed to them through actual images. The second point is very important, that is, why do modern people want to watch funny movies? Because you rarely appear as strong in life, but when watching funny movies, you always watch how the unified, brutal and coercive power comes to the plot and constantly pranks the victim in all kinds of way from the perspective of the strong and powerful character. You can follow the plot and react to its rhythm. When reacting, you feel that you are not working and at the same time, at a higher state where you can't reach in life, i.e. being strong and powerful, so you feel a complete release. This stimulation and reaction mechanism can be used without your self-conscious effort, so you feel a release when it is applied. This is we call escape. The greatest "advantage" of the escape is that it seems that you have escaped the burden of work in the leisure state, but it is this escape that makes you adapt to the next burden of work as soon as possible. So you enjoy watching funny movies. You can relax and sleep after the movie and go to work in high spirits the next day. If you watch a very heavy and serious movie, which seems to reveal something unspeakable, complicated, and inexplicable about human nature and leaves an open question that haunts you, how can you be prepared for work the next day? How can you reorganize your daily life according to the stimulation and reaction mechanism? Hence, leisure and entertainment is a way of "recharging", which refreshes you before you return to the life under a fixed working mechanism.

It should be emphasized here is that this kind of escape is strongly deceptive in nature, because it suppresses your desire by creating desire, and creates your desire for new products by suppressing your desire. In this way, all culture industry products do not satisfy demand, but suppress desire and continuously generate demand. This repression of desire and continuous generation of demand keep the production line of culture industry products rolling continuously and unceasingly, i.e. they need to be eternally renovated and constantly updated. However, none of the updates will not satisfy your desire, nor will it make your desire truly satisfied. Here is an example to explain why culture industry products are deceptive, although I think it does not quite hold water in the contemporary context. Imagine that the culture industry has completely gone bankrupt, say, all cinemas are closed, those who are most seriously affected are but only types of people in their time: the first type are housewives, and the second type is the homeless. Housewives do not have the separation between work and leisure, because they are always in the household. It looks like they never work but they are actually always at work. In this case, movies in the cinema are meaningless to her. She does not need to react spontaneously to movies and may not even have this ability, but as soon as the light in the cinema goes out and the screen lights up, the movie leads her into a realm that is nothing like her life. Therefore, the existence of cinemas really opens up a leisure world that is different from work for housewives, and the only difference between this leisure world and work is the total rupture. So if all cinemas are closed, housewives must be the real victim. In contrast, those who often go to the cinema for leisure are not really affected when cinemas shut down, because movies are not really helpful to them. The other type is the homeless. They come to a cinema to find a shelter from wind and rain, so the closure of cinemas is also a real loss in life for them. Horkheimer and Adorno use these two counterexamples to prove that culture industry products are only deceptive. However, modern people feel that they cannot live without culture industry products. This means that this stimulation and reaction mechanism not only needs to be continuously implemented at work, but also needs to be continuously hidden and covered up, so that people can still react to stimuli and feel that they are not working. Such a deceptive moment has become a necessity for those who grew up in the era after the flood of culture industry products. In the days of Horkheimer and Adorno, they did not reach this level, so they said that culture industry products are just a deception. When they saw people's fanaticism about culture industry products, they only said that the fanaticism was for nothing real but an illusory experience. But today, illusory experiences have become a necessity, which may not be anything they could have thought of in their time.

The entertainment Horkheimer and Adorno refer to is a double corruption of art and entertainment, because it is pre-arranged and intellectualized amusement, just like what we said about the so-called style–a stylized barbarism. As an effect calculated in advance, this entertainment is hidden in culture industry products beforehand. Here is an example that I always remember. Hollywood made a movie on how a comedy director films comedy. For him, a comedy that he puts his heart in is a precise, rhythmic performance. He stands behind the screen, perceiving how the audience react to his movie. Like a conductor, he knows exactly where there will be screams and where there will be laughs. If all these screams and laughs he expects can precisely burst out at the right time and at the right rhythm, it means that the movie is a success. This tells us that all entertainment is carefully fed through the rational mechanism. Without this technical rationality, it is not easy to make a comedy or thriller. How to feed the stimuli, how to anticipate reactions, how to arrange the rhythm when feeding stimuli beyond anticipated reactions...All these are highly concentrated calculative reason, and are not artistic creation at all. The highly concentrated calculative reason is an important reason for the corruption of entertainment here. In other words, as an audience, you have already been calculated. Just as workers on the production line have already been calculated by the machine, you as a viewer in front of the screen have also been calculated in advance by the information fed on the screen. In this sense you are a pure object. This is how Horkheimer and Adorno present the culture industry.

■

Related reading:
Chinese version: 马克斯·霍克海默，西奥多·阿道尔诺：《启蒙辩证法：哲学断片》，Shanghai People's Publishing House, p107-152; or English version: *Dialectic of Enlightenment: Philosophical Fragments*, Max Horkheimer/Theodor W. Adorno, Stanford University Press, p94-137.

青策充电站
联合主办：上海当代艺术博物馆、复旦大学哲学学院

工作团队
上海当代艺术博物馆：张琍莉、马慧婷、徐辰斐、邱鼎、黄彦娜
复旦大学哲学学院：袁新、林晖、沈奇岚、陈佳

实录册编辑团队
编辑：马慧婷、蔺佳
平面设计：邵君瑜
翻译：曾晨
校对：阮汇善

ECP Charging Station Programme
Co-organizers: Power Station of Art,
School of Philosophy, Fudan University

Programme Team
Power Station of Art: Zhang Lili, Ma Huiting, Xu Chenfei,
Qiu Ding, Huang Yanna
School of Philosophy, Fudan University: Yuan Xin, Lin Hui,
Shen Qilan, Chen Jia

Editorial Team
Editor: Ma Huiting, Lin Jia
Graphic Design: Shao Junyu
Translator: Zen Chen
Proofreader: Ruan Huishan

青策充电站
策展与艺术哲学
工作坊

实录

ECP Charging
Station
Workshop Series:
Curating and
Philosophy of Art

Record

以展览作为历史论述的主轴线，即将分析的重点放在艺术与公共之互动效应上，而"公共"所指的包括了政权、艺术体制、社会大众及社会公共空间等多个层次，而对近四十年的艺术来说，这个"公共"更既是本土的，也是全球的。艺术与公共之间的相互理解及期望如何影响艺术的发展？艺术的实践及观念如何响应、争取、妥协、抵抗、消解"公共"所给予的条件及难题？

资深艺术文献研究员、策展人翁子健将通过本次讲座给 1989 年至 2008 年之间中国当代艺术展览的条件及策略之演变勾勒出一个轮廓，以提示出研究及思考的出发点。讲座分时期地描述了中国当代艺术的展览的形势及发展脉络，继而选取其中一些有前瞻意义的展览，分析其动机、立场及所反映的议题，尽可能了解这些展览所涉及的种种政治，当中涉及多少精心布置的策略和不得已而为之的妥协，及对展览当时某些迫在眉睫的议题的强烈响应。

翁子健：
中国当代艺术
展览的历史
(1989—2008)

大家好，我是翁子健，原本我定下"中国当代艺术展览的历史(1989—2008)"这个题目，是想给大家讲特别标准的中国当代艺术展览史，后来，想到各位当中有一半是学哲学的，我将题目的方向略微转变了一下，变成"展览史和中国当代展览史"，希望通过中国，谈一点展览史的本体问题。

尽管对展览的研究由来已久，展览史被认定为一个独立的学科，却是最近的事。艺术史作为一种现代学科，在西方是 19 世纪正式确立的，其中，展览是作为研究艺术的诸多社会面貌中的一个分支。展览史在现代主义时期变得愈来愈重要，因为现代主义的进程中最关键的一次事件，正是 1863 年在法国出现的落选者沙龙。从那时起，展览变得越来越重要。

首先我想请大家思考一个问题：假设你要研究一个展览的历史，需要收集哪些资料。根据大家的热烈讨论，我们总结了以下这些要素，包括：社会背景；策展人、参展艺术家、主办方、场地；作品；现场图片等文献记录；媒体报道、评论；延伸活动；经费来源和赞助情况；同期展览；观众；展览结束之后，参展艺术家的后续发展、作品的去向(是否被收藏)、展览是否留下范式或模式这几个块面。

除了上述这些之外，我再补充几点。我们或许会通过采访艺术家和策展人来关注一些非常具体的问题。比如说："策展人去联系你的时候，对于这个展览他/她是怎么描述的？"这里面会存在一个落差，官方的策展论述与策展人跟艺术家的沟通不一定是一致的。很多时候我们采访艺术家，艺术家会跟我们说策展人根本没提展览是干嘛的，只是让他/她去参加。

另外我们会问的问题还有：展览的准备时间是多久；经费我们刚才提到了，除此之外还有许多具体的问题，比如运输、布展的方法、对建筑的改动等等。我们也会做文化政策的研究，展览举办城市的文化氛围往往对于展览的主题和开展的方式有着很大影响。文化政策相关的因素还包括了审查制度，有哪些作品是本来想展但最后没能展出的。历史上许多重要的展览都面临过这样的问题，因为意识形态或经费的原因没能实现原先的设想，因此对于一个展览里"妥协"的部分，我们也需要关注到。

展览并不仅仅是策展的问题，它是策展的观念经过了与艺术家、作品、主办方、观众、文化政策等很多因素交融后的结果。所以，它非常复杂，因而在当代艺术里也变得非常重要。因此我们在研究当代艺术的时候，很需要把这些政策、泛文化、经济的成分也考虑进去。另外刚才也有学员补充提到的，关于"野史"和"传说"的部分，即官方的记录和叙述之外的观察视角，也是一个值得被关注的角度。

那么，为何近20年里，展览史这个门类会愈来愈多受到重视，成为艺术史领域中一个特别重要的分支？这个问题没有正确答案，大家可以从不同的角度切入进行思考。

学员A："整个展览史表现出的是反传统、反权威、反体制在艺术身上的发酵过程，展览所代表的力量是具有社会性和大众性的一种体现。所以，展览史相较于过去包含在艺术史之内状态，它更可以单独成为一个门类，去表现艺术在不同的社会状态下，超出审美之外的力量。也就是说，正因为展览的社会意义或者是它回应和反映社会问题的这种功能越来越显著，它才会变得越来越重要。"

学员 B："你提出的这个问题有一个关键的时间界定，'近20年'，如果放在中国当代艺术发展的语境里来谈，在上世纪80年代末90年代初期，国内才逐渐开始有了'策展人'这一概念，而展览史的演进和'策展人'的发展是密不可分的。为什么策展人的身份会越来越重要，这可能需要考察社会历史背景，它跟这二十年间的文化史包括政治的走向都有着直接的联系。第二点就是跟现当代艺术在杜尚之后的发展有关，观念先行的艺术创作越来越抽象，策展人充当了观念的集中整理者，依托展览这一形式来进行表达。"

其实，不仅在中国国内，"策展人"这一概念在西方也一直经历定义上的变化。在很长一段时间里，"策展人"是美术馆或博物馆内管理和研究艺术品收藏的专职人员，直到1960年末，才慢慢出现比较明确的"独立策展人"这一概念，而正是独立策展人的出现让展览的性质产生了变化。如果我们去关注哈罗德·泽曼其人会发现，他之所以成为独立策展人，一个很有趣的原因是他当时被美术馆开除了，因此他不得不选择以这样一种方式继续做事。同时，由于观念艺术的兴起，也使展览在艺术的进程中变得愈来愈重要，从1960年代开始的去物质化运动，造成了一种对于艺术品的不信任的态度，人们渐渐发展出这样的观点：对艺术品的认知，似乎必须放在一个完整的论述里、一个展览里或者一种社会性的目光之下，才能形成有效的解读，艺术品本身不再说了算。

1.

由策展人撰写的展览研究型出版
物举例。图片源自翁子健讲义，
除特殊注明外本文内所有图片均
由讲者提供。

Examples of publications on exhibition
research written by curators. Images
from Anthony Wung's lecture slides. All
the images in this article are provided
by the speaker unless otherwise
specified.

另外一点，是人们越来越重视艺术在社会上的交流作用。当代艺术更多是交流的媒介，而不是美学的产品，而展览是提供交流的一个很重要的元素。所以说，展览史和当代艺术史是很难剥离开的。还有一个无法被忽视的背景，今天我们所处的时代是人类历史上展览的井喷时期，今天展览频繁发生的数量，是19世纪末20世纪初绝不可能媲美的。展览的绝对数量的增加和展览史在艺术史里的作用越来越重要是很有关系的。

此外，我们发现一个有趣的现象：现在，很多研究展览史的人，并不来自于传统意义上的艺术史家，反而往往是那些有意去做策展事业的人，也就是说，是策展人们在书写展览史。他们希望为"策展"这一专业树立一个"细目"，建立属于自己的历史。近二十年间，出现的很多展览史著作，都是由策展人撰写的，比如汉斯·乌尔里希·奥布里斯特所著的《策展简史》，他作为一名很有代表性的独立策展人，他很重要的一项成就是在展览史及策展史研究的推动上的。图示1，P6

英国的《AFTERALL》杂志出版了"展览史"系列书籍，也是这个领域的重要出版。它的结构是通过一本书还原一个展览，并且把一个展览作为研究的主体去展开。通过这样的工作，我们会逐渐建立一种类似于传统艺术史里叫作年表的东西：展览史里面最重要的时刻是什么？最重要的人物是哪些？

接着，我试着粗略地分析一下，在当下关于展览史的主流论述（即一种被策展主导的论述）中，一个展览被归入历史中、被认为具有历史重要性，大概是由于以下三个主要原因：第一，某个展览定义了某一艺术的理念、风格或媒介；第二，它标识出某一个重要的文化议题；第三，这个展览本身的形式具有独创性和影响力。这三点非常容易理解，也很容易描述，和美术史的逻辑相类似。我们来看一些具体的例子。

1. 定义了某一艺术的理念、风格、媒介的展览

首先介绍定义了某一艺术的理念、风格、潮流的展览。"当态度成为形式"是一个在展览史上一再被提及的展览。其实这个展览的完整题目是"活在你的头脑中：当态度成为形式（作品—观念—过程—情境—信息）"，看来它想处理的概念有很多。但是，从今天的角度去描述它的历史地位时，它才和观念主义思潮紧密相关，参展的艺术家中，很多都被艺术史定义为观念主义的重要人物，只要提到观念主义就会想到这个展览。图示2, P9

另一相似例子，是1966年在纽约犹太博物馆举办的展览"初级结构：年轻一代的美英雕塑家"，它比"当态度成为形式"还要早，我们现在所熟知的极简主义虽然不是这个展览的"发明"，但正是由于这个展览所引起的广泛关注才使得极简主义真正进入了人们的视野。图示3, P9

1985年，纽约现代艺术博物馆举办了"20世纪艺术中的'原始主义'：部落与现代之间的亲缘性"，当年这个展览受到了很多批评，引起了关于"原始艺术"和现代主义之间关系的激烈讨论，这种争论给展览带来的问题性也正是展览进入历史的重要原因。图示4, P9

当我们提到"关系美学"，我们必然会想到"交通展"（Traffic）。1996年在波尔多现代艺术博物馆举办的"交通展"是"关系艺术"这场理念运动里一个很重要的标志。图示5, P10

上述这些展览之所以成为历史的标杆，都是因为它跟某一艺术运动的定义或发展有直接的关系。在中国有哪些例子？我们比较容易想到的例子，有1993年的"后八九：中国新艺术"，因为通过这个展览人们知道了"政治波普"这一艺术潮流，尽管这一潮流

2.

左图：1969 年哈罗德·泽曼策划
的"当态度成为形式"展览现场。
右图：展览目录。

Left: Installation view of the exhibition,
"When Attitude Becomes Form", curated
by Harald Szeemann in 1969. Right:
Exhibition catalog.

3.

左图：1966 年卡尼斯顿·麦克
希恩策划的"初级结构"展览现
场，该展览标志着极简主义的兴
起。右图：展览海报。

Left: Installation view of the exhibition,
"Primary Structures", curated by Kynaston
McShine in 1966, which marks the rise of
Minimalism. Right: Exhibition poster.

4.

左图：1985 年展览"20 世纪艺术
中的原始主义：部落与现代之间的
亲缘性"在纽约现代艺术博物馆的
展览现场。右图：展览海报。

Left: Installation view of the exhibition
"'Primitivism' in 20th Century Art: Affinity
of the Tribal and the Modern" at MoMA,
New York, 1985. Right: Exhibition poster.

5.

1996年波尔多现代艺术博物馆
"交通展"展览现场。

Installation view of the exhibition,
"Traffic", CAPC, 1996.

6.

"后八九：中国新艺术"的展览海报及展览现场，香港艺术中心及香港大会堂，1993年。栗宪庭、张颂仁策展。

Poster and installation view of the exhibition "China's New Art, Post-1989" at Hong Kong Arts Centre and Hong Kong City Hall, 1993. Curated by Li Xianting and Zhang Songren.

7.

展览"对伤害的迷恋"中孙原＆彭禹的作品，中央美院雕塑创作工作室，2000年。栗宪庭策展。

Sun Yuan & Peng Yu's work at the exhibition "Obsession with Injury", Sculpture Creation Studio of Central Academy of Fine Arts, 2000. Curated by Li Xianting.

8.

黄永砅在"大地魔术师"展览现场布置作品。巴黎蓬皮杜艺术中心，1989年。

Huang Yongping installs his works at the exhibition "Magiciens de la Terre", Centre Pompidou, Paris, 1989.

9.

上图：顾德新作品在"大地魔术师"展览现场。下图：杨诘苍在其作品前。

Above: Gu Dexin's work at the exhibition "Magiciens de la Terre". Below: Yang Jiecang before his work.

不是由这个展览发明的。还有 1996 年在杭州举办的"现象·影像"，是这个展览，提出关于中国录像艺术的讨论。2000 年"对伤害的迷恋"是一个十分有趣的展览，它标识了"尸体艺术"这样一个虽短时间存在过，却十分重要的艺术倾向。图6、图示7, P11

2. 标识出某一文化议题

还有一种展览，它标识的是某一重要的文化议题。比如"大地魔术师"所涉及到的多元文化主义，我们讨论展览史的时候必然会讨论到这个展览，它在整个以西方为主导的文化论述里面补充了一个很重要块面。策展人让 - 于贝尔·马尔丹是当时蓬皮杜艺术中心的馆长。我觉得他是一个非常理想主义的人，他的想法是请100 位艺术家——其中 50 位是西方艺术家，50 位是非西方艺术家——共同参展，试图打破艺术史里长期以来以西方文化为中心且占主导的格局。但事实上，当所有的艺术家被放到这个展览里面，西方和非西方之间仍然有一个很明确的分裂，展览只加强这种区别性，而不能去磨灭它。图8、图示9, P12

"后人类"也是一个例子，这是 1992 至 1993 年的展览。我关注到近几年青策的展览也都说到了相关的问题，比如人工智能、赛博朋克。

这样一类有野心、有目的地去提出一个有关全球性宏大文化问题的展览，在中国历史上比较少。我觉得 2008 年的第三届广州三年展"向后殖民说再见"，是一个很有意思的案例。它提出了一条既关于中国又关于全球的重要思想线路，但是到目前为止关于这个展览的研究很少，我觉得很值得做深入的回顾与挖掘。图示10, P14

相比之下，中国关心本土文化议题的展览很多，我们在研究展览史时，这也是非常重要的一条脉络。1998 年在北京郊区举办的

10.

第三届广州三年展：与后殖民
说再见，策展人：高士明、张颂
仁、Sarat Maharaj。广东美
术馆，2008年。

The Third Guangzhou Triennial: Farewell
to Post-Colonialism, curated by Gao
Shiming, Zhang Songren, and Sarat
Maharaj, Guangdong Museum of Art, 2008.

11.

生存痕迹——'98中国当代艺术
内部观摩展，现时艺术工作室，
北京，1998年。

Traces of Existence—A Private Showing
of China Contemporary Art '98, Art Now
Studio, Beijing, 1998.

"生存痕迹"是一杰出例子。二十世纪九十年代以来，中国艺术家的活动范畴愈来愈走向城市边缘，而"生存痕迹"则是在城市边缘地带举办展览的一个前瞻性例子。这个展览是关于当时人普遍的生存状态，是关于"生活"，其中宋冬做了一个很有意思的作品，他制作了12缸酸菜给观众吃。这个作品马上让人联想到"交通展"，但由于"生存痕迹"在农民房子中发生，而"交通展"在美术馆内发生，宋冬的作品明显就带有更强的亲密感及真实感。图示11, P14

3. 独创而有影响力的展览形式

1997年起侯瀚如和小汉斯共同策划的巡回展览"移动中的城市"，是展览形式创新的重要例子。策展人让建筑师在美术馆或者展览场地里面设计一个结构，然后，让展览在这个结构里面发生。等于说美术馆先被改装一遍。展览的主题是东亚及东南亚的超级城市，所以，策展人希望展览现场象征一个生机勃勃的城市，具体的效果就是：很乱！展览中呈现的正是城市街道混乱的、野生的、有机的面貌。在"移动中的城市"之前，很少有展览会有目的地制造这么混乱的场景，传统上，被认为好的展览都是条理分明的，以艺术作品为绝对主角的。当时，"移动中的城市"受到的批评，正是它不尊重作品，展览观众分不清哪些是作品、哪些不是作品，也分不清哪个东西是哪个艺术家的作品，甚至还没有标签。图示12, P16

"移动中的城市"是典型的"强策展"，就是策展人创作成分很高的一个展览。相对应地，后来我们也有一种说法叫"弱策展"。这是一个有点吊诡的想法，既要策展又要策展很弱，不要去干预，让事情自然发生，用流行的话，就是"佛系策展"。其实，小汉斯做过另外一个项目叫"做"（do it），我觉得挺"佛系"的。从1993年开始，他邀请艺术家撰写方案，这些方案变成了一份份

12.

"移动中的城市"展览期刊及展览现场。

Exhibition magazine and installation view of "Cities on the Move".

13.

汉斯·乌尔里希·奥布里斯特自1993年起发起的项目"做",持续至今。

The project "do it", 1993 on wards. Initiated by Hans Ulrich Obrist.

14.

"后感性:狂欢"展览现场,北京电影学院,2001年。

Installation view of "Post-Perceptual: Carnival", Beijing Film Academy, 2001.

的说明书，后来他开始巡回这个展览，每到一处，即请人实现这些方案，同时继续收集新的方案。所以这项目就一直在持续成长，期间也会演变成不同的出版物。图示13，P16

我们再来看看在展览形式创新方面，中国展览史上有哪些案例。1980、1990年代的中国，中国实验艺术的展览很多是在"地下"发生的，因为"地上"的文化体系还没有完全承认现当代艺术。很多展览都是由艺术家自行组织的，在极为有限的条件下进行。当艺术家自行组织展览的时候，他们往往会把展览本身当成作品来创作，于是在这段时期，我们看到了由艺术家发明出的各种独具一格的展览形式。

在1999年，邱志杰和吴美纯在北京策划了一个很有观念野心的展览"后感性"，这个展览后来一共做了五、六次，成为了一个系列。第二次展览叫"狂欢"，2001年在北京电影学院举行。严格意义上来说，这次展览更像是一场多媒介表演。在规定的一个多小时内，现场同时发生各种各样的表演，包括很多即兴的行动。这个展览提出一个挑战，即它更明确地提出文献的有限性。这个展览非常强调感官的即时性体验。后来的人将如何在历史上描述这个展览？当然，可以采访那些亲临现场的人，但这个展览终归是在强调现场感受的不可重复性。图示14，P16

关于展览形式的发明，不得不提到徐震、唐茂宏、杨振中等艺术家2002年在上海做的"双胞胎展"即"范明珍和范明珠"。组织者找到一个空间，这个空间有两个完全对称的左右两边。在空间的入口，坐着一对双胞胎姐妹（即范明珍和范明珠本人），来者可以任意选择进入左边或右边的展场。两边展场，分别展览艺术家们的作品的两个版本，这两个版本很像，却有一些微妙的差别。

当然，我们也需要认识到，所谓展览的形式创新，也有不同的层面。"移动中的城市"和"做"的影响力或许会更深远一些，因为它所发明的形式，比如说和建筑师合作在美术馆内搭建新的展览空间，或者是利用"非空间"、以方案为主导进行的策展方法，这些创新是可以被沿用的，是可以在它们的基础上发生一些变奏的。它提出的是一些可持续发展的方向。在另一方面，后来者已经不太可能再做一次"双胞胎展"了，这些想法是不太可能被沿用的，当然，这个想法本身的创意和趣味，同样可以给人很大启发。

现在，我们可以来谈一下关于中国展览史的问题。我们刚才快速回顾的展览史，好像是一个全球展览史，它给我们一个这么印象，但是这个印象其实很大程度上是错误的。我们一定曾经看到过一些类似"世界上最重要的十个展览"或者"世界上最重要的十件艺术品"这样的论述，反复在主流的媒体出现。但是，其实这其中大家看到的大部分展览都是欧美的展览，它们来自欧美的文化语境。而当我们回顾中国展览史的时候，即发现很多展览及作品，是针对中国特有的问题，它们提出解决问题的办法，也似乎只有在中国的语境里面才能发生意义，才能被理解。这个时候，我们非常需要一些新的词汇，因为现有的大部份词汇是在西方语境中发明的。我们是否可以发明一些新的词汇，既能解释属于我们的文化语境，更能将我们创造的意义与全球领域沟通？

1989年在北京中国美术馆举办了"中国现代艺术展"，没有人会否认这个展览的重要性，但是这个展览的重要性在哪里呢？这个展览，是中国前卫艺术第一次能够在新中国成立以来最具有意识形态代表性的一个官方美术馆里面进行，很有颠覆性，而且很有时代意义。

这个展览在当时就出了名，很大程度上是因为在展览开幕那天发生了很有新闻性的事件。展览一共展出了300多件作品，来自

100多位艺术家，由一个组委会进行组织（没有个别策展人）。当时，一些艺术家及组委会成员，是希望把"八五新潮"以来的中国实验性艺术集中起来做一个回顾展，而且这个回顾展必须在中国美术馆做，因为他们考虑到中国美术馆的文化定位和政治含义很高，如果能在里面做这个展览，似乎就能确立中国实验艺术的合法性。

但是，在这100多人里面，不是所有人都抱有这样的想法，其中有些人，他们有不同的想法。他们并不想做这个展览，他们觉得不应该去官方的美术馆做，他们觉得这样是一种退步。他们认为实验艺术是激进的，是颠覆文化基建的事，不应该与固有的文化体制合作。这些艺术家也参展了这个展览，但是他们的作品，不是为了把展览做好，他们是为了批评，甚至毁掉这个展览。这个展览有趣的地方在于，它不像我们之前说到的很多展览，很统一，大家带着合作的姿态去共同描述一个主题。在这个展览里有很大的冲突，有不同的意见。

当时，中国美术馆同意他们做这个展览不是以主办方名义，而是仅仅提供了场地租赁，并且只在农历新年期间限时出租两个星期，同时还设定了一些条件，包括作品中不能有裸体及政治题材等，最重要的一点，是不能有现场的行为艺术。然而，当那些想毁掉这个展览的艺术家听到这个消息，想必是肯定会做行为艺术的。于是开幕那天，便发生了一系列著名的行为介入。艺术家肖鲁在官方名义上参展的作品是一个名为《对话》的装置作品，其造型是两个相邻的电话亭，上有一男一女在通话的图像。开幕现场，她突然拿出一把手枪，向她自己的作品开枪，打碎了电话亭上面的玻璃。问题严重了！她在一个人头拥挤的公共场合里开枪了，警察马上就出动了。也是因为这个行为，展览被迫关停了6天。这个事情成了新闻猛料，国内外媒体都进行了报道。于是，关于这个展览便有了两个层次的冲突，第一重冲突是展览

15.

1989年2月5日，"中国现代艺术大展"在中国美术馆开幕。开幕当天，艺术家肖鲁对准自己的作品连开两枪。

On February 5, 1989, the "China/Avant-Garde Exhibition" opened at the National Art Museum of China. Artist Xiao Lu fired at her work twice on the opening day.

的参加者之间的冲突，而第二重冲突就是前卫艺术跟社会主流意见之间的冲突。当时的公众对这个展览批评意见很大：前卫艺术都是做这么荒诞的事情吗？另外就是作品的内容和形式上，既不好看，也不写实，当时的中国观众十分不习惯。这个展览出了各种各样的问题，也造成了后来在很长一段时间里，中国所有官方展览机构完全禁止装置、录像、行为艺术等非统媒介的作品的展出。地面上的艺术机构，在几乎整个1990年代里都是不能出现这样的展览的。图示15, P20

这个展览，应该很难说是一个"好"展览。展览出了很多乱子，后来还一度因为收到炸弹威胁被迫暂停了第二次。想为前卫艺术争取合法性的那一拨人很生气，认为倾尽心力做的展览，被这样破坏掉，很可惜。我认为，上述的这种意见分裂，这种对中国当代艺术的文化立场的两种意见，一直是中国当代艺术的发展上的显要问题。应该合作、平和？还是应该更激进、更地下？

有趣的是，2000年的时候又发生过一次针对这个意见冲突的标志性事件。那就是2000年的第三届上海双年展。对于中国来说，它是一个有划时代意义的展览，因为它是中国第一个国际性当代艺术双年展。在2000年做一个国际性的大展，那个难度是我们现在很难想象的。比如说，当时国内的美术馆根本不知道怎么把作品从国外运输过来，他们从没用过国际的运输公司。有一些录像作品，他们也不知道该怎么展示。所以，当时领导上海美术馆的人，是非常勇敢的，做了一件很了不起的事。而且，他们还承受了来自上层领导的压力，就是中国官方的文化系统。当时，人们并不知道做这样一个国际性的展览到底是好还是不好——一方面当时非常担心，不知道会否有坏的影响，另一方面又跃跃欲试，因为2000年的时候中国正在一步步走向国际化，而且上海其实是一个很

16.

第三届上海双年展"海上·上海"的举办地上海美术馆外的景象，2000年。

The scene outside the Shanghai Art Museum where the third Shanghai Biennale "Shanghai Spirit" was held, 2000.

 17.

《沙的银行或银行的沙》，黄永砯，2000年上海双年展现场，上海美术馆。

Bank of Sand or Sand of Bank, Huang Yongping, Shanghai Biennale 2000, Shanghai Art Museum.

理想的试点，它有着国际大都会的历史背景。图示16, P22

这是老的上海美术馆，它是一个英式风格的建筑，是旧上海跑马场的总部，所以在这个地方做展览，因为建筑结构的问题，其实不太容易。我们看到的这件是黄永砯的作品《沙的银行或银行的沙》，用沙子做成外滩汇丰银行老建筑的模型，他的理想是沙子造成的银行会在展览的过程中慢慢塌下来。据我的调查，由于作品做得太好了，最终没能塌下来。图示17, P22

这是唯一一个不在美术馆现场展览的作品，来自日本艺术家河原温的日期画《今天》系列，他当时的想法就是把它们挂在一个幼儿园里面，但是又不告诉老师和小朋友这是什么，他们和作品在一个空间里，照常上课。图示18, P24

这届上海双年展研讨会的题目很明确，叫"海上·上海——一种特殊的现代性"，明显是想藉由展览，重提上海曾经是国际大都会的历史图示19, P24。1920、1930年代，上海是世界上顶尖的大都会，但是由于历史原因，它没有继续在这个轨道上前行。当中国再一次跟世界接轨，重新讨论上海的现代性，其文化政治目的不言而喻。当然，绝大部分的作品，其实是跟这个主题没有关系的。各种作品一起展览，彼此之间也没法交流，这是因为展览里有很多不同的力量，有四个策展人，而四个策展人又有不同的目的和策略。但是，总体而言，这个展览最重要的意义就是它的官方背景，一个官方机构在努力举办当代艺术的而且是国际范围的当代艺术展览，这一定程度上延续了1989年的"中国现代艺术展"的那第一拨人的愿望：在中国建立一个合法的土壤，让实验艺术平和地、安全地生长和展示。而跟1989年不一样的是，在2000年，那些持激进意见的另一拨人，这次他们没有挤进去同一个展览，他们在另外的地点做自己展览，选择在同一个时间开幕。这些展览中，立场最鲜明的是"不合作方式"。当时上海非

18.

河原温的作品参展第三届上海双
年展期间在上海某幼儿园内进行
展出。

On Kawara's work exhibited in a
kindergarten in Shanghai during the
third Shanghai Biennale.

19.

"海上·上海———一种特殊的现
代性"2000年上海双年展研讨
会现场。

Symposium of the Shanghai Biennale
"Shanghai Spirit——A Special Modernity",
2000.

20.

"不合作方式"展览现场，
2000年。

Installation view of "Noncooperation
Mode", 2000.

21.

"不合作方式"展览现场，艺术
家杨志超的行为艺术作品《种
草》，2000年。

Yang Zhichao's performance art,
Planting Grass, at the exhibition "Fuck
Off", 2000.

22.

"不合作方式"展览现场，
2000年。

Installation view of "Noncooperation
Mode", 2000.

官方的展览空间很少，组织者与当时上海少有的几家画廊之一东廊画廊合作，使用了东廊在苏州河畔的仓库里进行了这次展览。共有 47 位艺术家参展。^{图示20，P25}

按照策展人的说法，所谓"不合作方式"是一种态度。当实验艺术被官方机构接受以后，它就会失去它的积极性，失去它的活力。为了保持创造性，艺术家必须主动地生活在边缘、走在边缘。我们看到这个展览展出的作品，跟同时发生的双年展内展览的很不一样。我们刚才提到过的展览"对伤害的迷恋"，也提及了 2000 年的时候中国存在过一个短暂的艺术倾向，艺术家关注死亡、暴力、伤害。用人体或动物标本为材料，这些作品都在"不合作方式"中有所呈现。这是艺术家杨志超的行为艺术作品《种草》，他在展览现场临时搭了手术台，请外科医生在自己的身上种了一棵草^{图示21，P25}。展览上，还有一个传说：艺术家朱昱做了一个备受极大争议的作品，策展人很纠结到底要不要展这个作品，最后决定不展，但是展览现场有一个黑色的箱子。传说中这件作品就在这个黑色箱子里面。

这是我的最后一张图，"不合作方式"的现场。照片上有两件我个人非常喜欢的作品：后面是孟煌的画，前面是孙原的作品。^{图示22，P26}

谢谢大家！　　　　　　　　　　　　　　　■

To use exhibitions as the central axis for a historical discourse means to emphasize the interactions between art and the "public," in which "public" refers to a complex of political authorities, art institutions, the general public, the public social sphere, and more. Moreover, especially for art of recent decades, this "public" is both local and global. How does art and "public" understand each other, what do they anticipate from each other, and how does this relationship affect the development of art? How do the conceptual and material practices of art respond, negotiate, make compromises, resist, and resolve the questions, problems, and conditions given by the "public"?

This lecture brought by Anthony Yung, a senior researcher on art archives and a curator, aims to sketch the changing circumstances and instrumental and critical understanding of exhibition in the realm of contemporary Chinese art between 1989 and the late 2000s. It periodizes the history of exhibition-making in contemporary Chinese art and describes its general conditions and contexts. We will look closer at these landmark exhibitions to analyze their motivations and the issues that they reflect. We will attempt to understand the pre-condition for exhibition criticism is a general understanding of the different politics involved in exhibitions: what were the intentions and what were the strategies? What were the constraints and reluctantly made compromises? What were the problems at stake that artists and curators attempted to respond to?

Anthony Yung:
A Critical Review of the Exhibition History of Contemporary Chinese Art, 1989-2008

Hello, everyone. I'm Anthony Yung. The original title of my speech is "A Critical Review of the Exhibition History of Contemporary Chinese Art, 1989-2008", under which I was about to talk the exhibition history in a textbook way. Yet, it later came to me that half of you are majored in philosophy, so I have changed the orientation slightly into "History of Exhibitions and Exhibition History of Contemporary Chinese Art", and am going to talk about the noumenon of exhibition history through China.

Although people started to study exhibitions long time ago, only recently has exhibition history been identified as an independent discipline. Art history was officially established as a modern discipline in the West in the 19th century, and exhibition history is one of its branches that study the many social aspects of art. Exhibition history has become increasingly important during the movement of Modernism, thanks to the most crucial event in the course, Salon des Refusés, which took place in France in 1863. Since then, exhibitions have become more and more important.

First, I would like to ask you a question: if you are going to study the history of an exhibition, what information do you need to collect? After the heated discussion, here is a summary of the key aspects, i.e. social context; curators, participating artists, organizers, venues; works; documents including pictures of installation views; media coverage and reviews; extended activities; funding sources and sponsorship; concurrent exhibitions; audience; future development of participating artists after an exhibition, whereabouts of works (whether they are collected), and whether the exhibition provides a paradigm or pattern.

In addition to what is mentioned above, I would like to add another few points. We may focus on some highly specific questions when interviewing the artists and the curator, e.g. "When the curator reached out to you, how did s/he describe this exhibition?" There may be a gap and inconsistency between the official curatorial discourse and the curator's communication with artists. In an interview, we are often told by an artist that the curator invites him/her to participate without mentioning the purpose of the exhibition.

Another question we may ask is, how long does it take to prepare an exhibition? Apart from funding which we just mentioned, there are other specific issues such as transportation, methods of installation, and changes to the building. We also research on cultural policies, as the cultural atmosphere of the city where the exhibition is held often has a great influence on the theme and the actualization of the exhibition. Factors related to cultural policies include censorship, e.g. which works were planned to be exhibited but were cancelled in the end? Many important exhibitions in history suffered the same fate and deviated from the original plan for ideological or financial reasons. Therefore, we also need to pay attention to the "compromise" made in curating an exhibition.

Exhibition is not just about curating. Instead, it is the result of the curatorial concept mixing with artists, works, organizers, viewers, cultural policies and many other factors. Therefore, it is a very complicated and very important part of contemporary art. Thus, when studying contemporary art, we need to take these policies, cross-cultural, and economic factors into consideration. "Unofficial history" and "hearsay" mentioned by a participant just now is a perspective beyond official records and narratives, and one that is worthy of attention.

Then, why has exhibition history been receiving more and more attention in the past 20 years, and has become an important branch of art history? There is no standard answer to this question, and everyone can think about it from different perspectives.

Participant A: The exhibition history demonstrates how anti-tradition, anti-authoritarianism, and anti-system amplify in art, and that the power of exhibition embodies its nature of sociality and publicity. Therefore, compared with the times when exhibition history fell under art history, it has become an independent category for presenting the power of art under different social conditions beyond aesthetics. That is to say, the exhibition history has become increasingly important because of the social significance of exhibitions or how exhibitions respond to and reflect social issues.

Participant B: There is a key time frame of the question you raised, "the last 20 years". In the context of the development of Chinese contemporary art, the concept of "curator" started to emerge in China in the late 1980s and early 1990s, which is closely linked to the evolution of exhibition history. To understand why the role of curators has become more and more important, first we need to review the social and historical background during this specific period, which is directly connected with the cultural history and political trends in the last two decades. Second, the rise of curators is also a result of the development of modern and contemporary art after Marcel Duchamp. As concept-first artworks become more and more abstract, curators act as the organizer of concepts and express them in the form of exhibitions.

In fact, outside China, the concept of "curator" has also been given a new definition in the West. For a long time, a "curator" was a full-time staff member who managed and researched art collections in art museums or museums. It was not until the end of 1960 that a relatively clear concept of "independent curator" gradually came into light, and it was independent curators that changed the nature of exhibition. If we look at the story of Harald Szeemann, one of the interesting reasons why he became an independent curator is that he was fired by the museum, so he had to continue his work in another way. At the same time, the rise of conceptual art has also made exhibitions more and more important during the development of art. The dematerialization movement that began in the 1960s has created distrust in works of art, and people have come to this view: it seems that the perception of artworks must be placed in a complete discourse, an exhibition, or a social perspective in order to form an effective interpretation, while artworks themselves no longer dominate.

Moreover, people increasingly recognize the role of art in social communication. Contemporary art is more a medium of communication than an aesthetic product, and exhibitions are an important element in providing communication. Therefore, it is difficult to separate the history of exhibitions from the history of contemporary art. Besides, there is also the background that cannot be ignored, i.e. the times we are living in witnesses an explosion of exhibitions that is unprecedented in human history. The current frequency of exhibitions is incomparable to that in the end of the 19th century and the beginning of the 20th century. The increase in the absolute number of exhibitions is related to the increasing importance of exhibition history in the field of art history.

In addition, we have seen an interesting phenomenon. Nowadays, many people who study the history of exhibitions are not art historians in the traditional sense, but those who intend to curate. That is to say, it is curators that are writing exhibition history. Curators hope to build a detailed classification for "curating" as a specialty and create their own history. In the past two decades, many books on exhibition history have been written by curators, such as *A Brief History of Curating by Hans Ulrich Obrist.* As a representative independent curator, one of his significant achievements is that he has promoted the studies of exhibition history and history of curating. Fig. 1, P6

The English journal *Afterall* published the *Exhibition Histories* book series, which is another important publication in the field of exhibition history. In this series, each book is designed to revive an exhibition, with the exhibition as the object of research. Through work like this, we can gradually build something similar to the chronology of traditional art history: what are the most important moments in the history of exhibitions? Who are the most important figures?

Next, I'm going to briefly analyze three types of exhibitions that are recognized as historically important according to the current mainstream, a curating-led discourse on exhibition history: first, exhibitions that define an artistic concept, style or medium; second, exhibitions that identify an important cultural issue; and third, exhibitions that have an original and influential form. These three types are easy to understand and describe, and are similar to the logic of art history. Now, let's look at some specific examples.

i. Exhibitions that define an artistic concept, style or medium

First, exhibitions that define an artistic concept, style and trend. The exhibition "When Attitude Becomes Form" has been repeatedly referred to in exhibition history. In fact, the full title of this exhibition is "Live in Your Head: When Attitudes Become Form (Works—Concepts—Processes—Situations—Information)", which tells the many concepts it wants to work with. However, when describing its place in history from the modern perspective, it starts to closely relate to Conceptualism. Many of the participating artists in this exhibition are defined as important figures of conceptualism in art history. Whenever people talk about Conceptualism, this exhibition will come to their mind. Fig. 2, P9

Another similar example is the exhibition "Primary Structures: Younger American and British Sculptors" held at the Jewish Museum in New York City in 1966, prior to "When Attitude Becomes Form". Although Minimalism that is well known now, is not the "invention" of this exhibition, it is precisely because of the extensive attention this exhibition has caused that Minimalism has entered people's horizons. Fig. 3, P9

In 1985, the exhibition "'Primitivism' in 20th-Century Art: Affinity of the Tribal and the Modern" was held at the Museum of Modern Art (MoMA) in New York City. The exhibition drew much criticism and caused intense debate about the relationship between "primitive art" and Modernism at that time. Such debate gave the exhibition a problematic nature, which is an important reason why it has gone down in history. Fig. 4, P9

When talking about "Relational Aesthetics", we will definitely think of "Traffic". This exhibition held at the Museum of Contemporary Art of Bordeaux (CAPC) in 1996 is a significant marker of the conceptual movement of "Relational Art". Fig. 5, P10

The above-mentioned exhibitions have become a historical benchmark because they are directly related to the definition or development of an art movement. What examples do we have in China? One example that we can easily think of is "China's New Art, Post-1989", because people get to know the artistic trend of "political pop" through this exhibition, although this trend is not invented by this exhibition. Another example is the exhibition "Image and Phenomena" held in Hangzhou in 1996, which proposes a discussion on Chinese video art. The "Obsession with Injury" in 2000 is a very interesting exhibition, because it marks the artistic tendency of "corpse art", which existed only for a short period of time but had such great importance. Fig. 6 & Fig. 7, P11

ii. Exhibitions that identify a cultural issue

Then there are exhibitions that identify an important cultural issue. For example, multiculturalism addressed in the exhibition "Magicians of the Earth", which comes up every time when we discuss exhibition history, and it complements the western-led cultural discourse with an important aspect. This exhibition was curated by Jean-

Hubert Martin, then director of the Centre Pompidou. I think he is very idealistic. His idea is to invite 100 participating artists, including 50 Western artists and 50 non-Western artists, in an attempt to change the landscape of art history that had been centered around and dominated by Western culture. However, despite all the artists were featured in this exhibition, there was still a very clear division between the West and the non-West, and the exhibition only strengthened this distinction, instead of eliminating it. Fig. 8 & Fig. 9, P12

Another example is the exhibition "Post Human" (1992-1993). I have noticed that the exhibitions of Emerging Curator's Project in recent years have taken on similar topics, such as artificial intelligence and cyberpunk.

Such ambitious and purposeful exhibitions that raise a grand global cultural issue are rare in Chinese history. To me, the "Farewell to Post-Colonialism" at the Third Guangzhou Triennial in 2008 is an interesting case, because it puts forward an important thread of thought on both China and the world, but there has been very little research on this exhibition. I think it is worthy of further review and exploration. Fig. 10, P14

In contrast, there are many exhibitions in China that concern local cultural issues. This is also a very important context in the study of exhibition history. "Trace of Existence" held in the suburbs of Beijing in 1998 is an outstanding example. Since the 1990s, Chinese artists' scope of activities has gradually shifted to the edge of the city, and "Trace of Existence" is a forward-looking example of holding exhibitions on the edge of the city. This exhibition is about people's general living conditions at that time, and about "life". Among others, Song Dong made a very interesting work. He made 12 large pots of pickled cabbage for the audience, and this work immediately reminds me of Traffic. However, "Traces of Existence" took place in a farmer's house while Traffic took place in the art museum. In this way, Song Dong's work obviously delivers a stronger sense of intimacy and realism. Fig. 11, P14

iii . Exhibitions that are original and influential

The traveling exhibition "Cities on the Move" co-curated by Hou Hanru and Hans Ulrich Obrist since 1997 is a significant example of formal innovation of exhibitions. The curators asked the architect to design a structure in the art museum or exhibition venue, and then let the exhibition take place in this structure. That is to say, the museum was refitted beforehand. The exhibition is themed on supercities of East and Southeast Asia, so the curators want to use the installation view to symbolize a vibrant city. The actual effect is: very messy! What is on display is the chaotic, wild and organic look of city streets. Prior to "Cities on the Move", few exhibitions would purposely create such chaotic scenes. Traditionally, what is considered a good exhibition is well-organized, with art works as the absolute protagonist. At that time, "Cities on the Move" was criticized precisely for not respecting the works. Viewers could not tell which things were works and which were not; nor could they distinguish the artist of a specific work, because all works were not labelled. ^{Fig. 12, P16}

"Cities on the Move" is a typical example of "strong curation", which contains much creation by the curator. Correspondingly, later there is also "weak curation", which is somewhat paradoxical because it requires curators to curate without invention and let things occur naturally. Put in buzzword, it is *Foxi* (literally 'Buddhist-style', means unambitious and peaceful) curation. Speaking of which, Hans Ulrich Obrist also curated a project called "do it", which I think is quite *Foxi*. Since 1993, Obrist has been inviting artists to write down their plans, and compiling them into a manual. Later, he began to tour the exhibition. Everywhere he goes, he asks people to implement the written plans, while continuing to collect new ones. In this way, this project keeps growing, and comes out as different publications. ^{Fig. 13, P16}

Now let's see what cases of innovation in exhibition forms we have in Chinese exhibition history. In the 1980s and 1990s in China, many exhibitions of experimental art took place "underground", because the "ground" cultural system had not fully recognized modern and contemporary art. Many exhibitions were organized by artists themselves and implemented under very limited conditions. When organizing an exhibition on their own, artists often created the exhibition like their work. During this period, we saw various unique exhibition forms invented by artists.

In 1999, Qiu Zhijie and Wu Meichun curated a

conceptual and ambitious exhibition "Post-Perceptual" in Beijing. Later, they curated another five or six exhibitions under the same theme as a series. The second exhibition, "Carnival", was held at the Beijing Film Academy in 2001. Strictly speaking, this exhibition is more like a multi-media performance. In the given more than one hour, a variety of performances were staged simultaneously, including many impromptu actions. This exhibition posed a challenge by explicitly addressing the limits of documents, and placed great emphasis on the immediate experience of the senses. How will people describe this exhibition in history in the future? You can certainly interview those who were in the exhibition room, but this exhibition is designed to emphasize the non-repeatability of firsthand feelings after all. Fig. 14, P16

When it comes to the invention of exhibition forms, I have to mention the "twin exhibition", "Fan Mingzhen and Fan Mingzhu", curated by artists such as Xu Zhen, Tang Maohong, and Yang Zhenzhong in Shanghai in 2002. The organizer found a space with two perfectly symmetrical chambers on left and right sides. At the entrance of the space sat the twin sisters, Fan Mingzhen and Fan Mingzhu. Visitors could choose to enter the left or the right exhibition room. The two rooms showcased two versions of the artists' works, which have many similarities and some nuances.

Besides, we should recognize that the innovation of exhibition forms takes place on different levels. The exhibitions "Cities on the Move" and "do it" may have more profound influence, because of the forms they have invented, such as working with the architect to create new exhibition space in the museum, or using "non-space" project-led curatorial methods. Their innovations can be adopted by other people and variations can be made based on them, as the exhibitions have proposed some directions of sustainable development. In contrast, it is not likely that latecomers are going to curate another "twin exhibition", which means the ideas of this exhibition will not be reused. Nevertheless, the creativity and fun of the idea itself can also be very enlightening.

Now let's talk about Chinese exhibition history. The exhibition history we just recapped on seems to be the history of global exhibitions. It gives us such an impression, but this impression is wrong to a large extent. We must have seen recurring remarks like "the ten most important exhibitions in the world" or "the ten most important artworks in the world" in the mainstream media. However, most of these exhibitions are from a European or American cultural context. Looking back at Chinese exhibition history, we find that many Chinese exhibitions and works focus on issues exclusive to China, and the solutions they propose are only meaningful and understandable in the Chinese context. At this point, we need new vocabulary, because most of the existing vocabulary has been invented in the Western context. Can we invent new words that can not only explain our own cultural context but also communicate the meaning we create to the global realm?

In 1989, the "China/Avant-Garde Exhibition" was held

at the National Art Museum of China in Beijing. No one would deny the importance of this exhibition, but what is so important about this exhibition? Being the first Chinese avant-garde art exhibition held in a state-owned art museum—the epitome of the country's ideology—since the founding of new China, it is revolutionary and epoch-making.

This exhibition was already famous when it was held, largely because of a news event on the opening day. The exhibition featured more than 300 works from more than 100 artists, arranged by an organizing committee (without individual curators). At that time, some artists and members of the organizing committee wanted to hold a retrospective of Chinese experimental art since the '85 New Wave in no other place but the National Art Museum of China, because they thought the museum has high cultural positioning and political significance, and the retrospective may legitimize Chinese experimental art if held in this museum.

However, not all of the 100 artists agreed, and some had different ideas. They didn't want to participate in this exhibition, because they didn't think the exhibition should be organized by a state-owned art museum, and saw it as a step backward. In their view, experimental art is radical and subversive of cultural infrastructure, and should not work with the inherent cultural system. Finally, these artists still participated in this exhibition. However, their works are not for the good of the exhibition, but to criticize or even sabotage the exhibition. What's interesting is that unlike the many exhibitions we have talked about, where everyone was unified and worked together to depict a common theme, there were major conflicts and disagreements in this exhibition.

In fact, the National Art Museum of China agreed to this exhibition not as an organizer, but as a lessor of the venue. The museum only allow the use of venue for two weeks during the Lunar New Year with strict conditions, including no nudity or political themes, and mostly importantly, no live performance art. However, when those artists who intended to destroy this exhibition heard about this, they must have decided to go for performance art. Hence, on the opening day, a series of famous behavioral interventions took place. Artist Xiao Lu's work is officially known an installation called *Dialogue*, which is about two adjacent telephone booths with the images of a man and a woman talking on the phone. At the opening scene, she suddenly took out a pistol and fired at her own work, smashing the glass of the phone booths. It was serious! She fired in a crowded public place, and the police were immediately out. Because of her behavior, the exhibition was forced to close for 6 days. This incident went viral on domestic and foreign media. As a result, there are two levels of conflicts in this exhibition. The first conflict is between the participating artists, and the second is between avant-garde art and the mainstream. The public was highly critical of the exhibition: should avant-garde art be about such ridiculous things? In addition, the content and form of the works were neither pleasant to look at nor realistic, and therefore, appeared strange to the Chinese audience. All kinds of problems arose in this exhibition, which later caused all state-owned exhibition institutions in China to completely ban the exhibition of works in the form of unconventional media such as installations, videos, and performance art. No art institutions on the ground could hold such exhibition throughout the 1990s. [Fig. 15, P20]

This exhibition could hardly be called a "good" exhibition. There were a lot of troubles in the exhibition, and it was suspended for a second time because of the bomb threat. Those who wanted to legitimize avant-garde art was furious, thinking it was a shame to spoil the exhibition like this which they had put their heart in. I think the above-mentioned divided opinions represent the two cultural standpoints of Chinese contemporary art, and have always been a significant issue during the development of Chinese contemporary art. Should they cooperate and make peace, or should they be more radical and underground?

It is interesting to note that in 2000, another emblematic incident occurred due to the same conflict, that is, the third Shanghai Biennale in 2000. For China, it is an epoch-making exhibition because it is the country's first international biennial of contemporary art. The difficulties in curating an international exhibition in 2000 are beyond our imagination, e.g. domestic art museums did not know how to transport works from abroad, because they had never worked with an international transportation company, and they did not know how to display some video works. Under such circumstances, the team who directed the Shanghai Art Museum were very brave and did a great job under pressure from their superiors, that is, China's official cultural system. At that time, people were not sure if it was good to have such an international exhibition. On the one hand, they were anxious and uncertain if it would have a bad effect, yet on the other hand, they were eager to give it a try, because China was on the way to internationalization in 2000, and Shanghai was an ideal pilot with the historical background as an international metropolis. Fig. 16, P22

This is the old Shanghai Art Museum, a British-style architecture and the headquarters of the former Shanghai Racecourse. It is not easy to stage an exhibition here because of the architectural structure. Here is the work by Huang Yongping, *Bank of Sand or Sand of Bank*, which uses sand to model the old building of HSBC Bank on the Bund. Ideally, he wanted the sand bank to slowly collapse during the exhibition, however as far as I know, it was too well made to collapse in the end. Fig. 17, P22

This is the only work that was not displayed in the art museum. It is the date painting series by the Japanese artist, On Kawara, *Today*. He wanted to show the paintings in a kindergarten, without telling the teachers and children what they were, so the teachers and children had classes as usual in the same space with his work. Fig. 18, P25

The symposium of the third Shanghai Biennale has a

very clear theme, "Shanghai Spirit-A Special Modernity", apparently intending to revisit the history of Shanghai as an international metropolis through the exhibition. [Fig. 19, P24] In the 1920s and 1930s, Shanghai was the world's top metropolis, but it did not continue on this track for historical reasons. When China set out again on the way of internationalization, the cultural and political purpose of re-discussing Shanghai's modernity was self-evident. Nevertheless, most of the works had nothing to do with this theme. Various works were exhibited together with no way of communicate, because there were four different curators who had different goals and strategies in the exhibition. However, this exhibition is important mostly because of its state-owned background, i.e. a state-owned institution trying to organize an international contemporary art exhibition. To some extent, it continues the aspiration of the people who put on the first contemporary art exhibition, "China/Avant-Garde Exhibition" of 1989, that is to establish a legal ground in China for experimental art to grow and display peacefully and safely. Yet unlike in 1989, another group of people with radical opinions did not pile themselves into the Shanghai Triennial 2000, but chose to hold their own exhibitions at other locations concurrently with the Shanghai Triennial. Among all these exhibitions, the one with the clearest stance is "Fuck Off" (The Incooperative Approach). There were very few private exhibition spaces in Shanghai. The organizer of "Fuck Off" cooperated with Eastlink Gallery, one of the few galleries in Shanghai at the time, and staged the exhibition in Eastlink Gallery's warehouse on the Suzhou River. It was attended by a total of 47 participating artists.[Fig. 20, P25]

According to the curator, the "noncooperation mode" is an attitude. When accepted by official institutions, experimental art will lose its enthusiasm and vitality. In order to remain creative, artists must take the initiative to live and walk on the edge. We can see that the works exhibited in this exhibition are very different from those in the concurrent third Shanghai Biennale. We mentioned the exhibition "Obsession with Injury" earlier, and talked about the short-term artistic tendency in China in 2000 when artists paid attention to death, violence and injury, and used human or animal specimens as creation materials. Similar works were presented in "Fuck Off". Here is Yang Zhichao's performance art work Planting Grass. He temporarily sets up an operating table at the exhibition and asks the surgeon to plant a grass on his body Fig. 21, P25. There is a hearsay about the exhibition that artist Zhu Yu made a highly controversial work, and the curator could not decide to show this work or not at first and finally decided not to. There was a black box at the exhibition, where it was said the work was.

Here is the last picture of my speech, the installation view of "Fuck Off". There are two works in this photo that I personally like a lot: Meng Huang's painting in the behind, and Sun Yuan's work in the front Fig. 22, P26.

Thank you!

青策充电站
联合主办：上海当代艺术博物馆、复旦大学哲学学院

工作团队
上海当代艺术博物馆：张琍莉、马慧婷、徐辰斐、邱鼎、黄彦娜
复旦大学哲学学院：袁新、林晖、沈奇岚、陈佳

实录册编辑团队
编辑：马慧婷、蔺佳
平面设计：邵君瑜
翻译：曾晨
校对：阮汇善

ECP Charging Station Programme
Co-organizers: Power Station of Art,
School of Philosophy, Fudan University

Programme Team
Power Station of Art: Zhang Lili, Ma Huiting, Xu Chenfei,
Qiu Ding, Huang Yanna
School of Philosophy, Fudan University: Yuan Xin, Lin Hui,
Shen Qilan, Chen Jia

Editorial Team
Editor: Ma Huiting, Lin Jia
Graphic Design: Shao Junyu
Translator: Zen Chen
Proofreader: Ruan Huishan

青策充电站
策展与艺术哲学
工作坊

实录

ECP Charging
Station
Workshop Series:
Curating and
Philosophy of Art

Record

什么是策展？为什么策展？策展作为职业包括哪些要求？如何看待策展与艺术写作、学术研究的关系？目前策展中最大的阻力是什么？独立策展的出路在哪里？……

策展并不是一个新兴职业，身处今天这一特殊的艺术时代，策展面临着空前的压力、挑战和机遇。作为策展人，将如何应对这一新的变化，并如何能始终保持对这份职业的狂热和激情？带着这些疑问，本次讲座围绕近年来国内外的一些重要展览（包括讲者本人策划的几个展览），就相关问题作了一些尝试性的讨论。

鲁明军：
策展及其能
动性与政治
力

谢谢 PSA 的邀请，也感谢沈语冰和沈奇岚老师！很高兴有这样一个机会，跟大家分享一些关于策展的认识、经验和体会。策展和理论思考、学术研究不太一样，不是说你越年长就做得越好，有时可能恰恰相反，越年轻反而越敏锐，反而越有行动力。所以，我其实也是抱着学习的心态，来这里和大家交流的。

为什么策展？

首先，我想还是回到一个基本的问题：什么是策展。想必在座的各位都有自己的定义和理解，我们也不难在相关专业书籍中找到各种不同的解释。我自己的理解是，和"当代"这个词一样，"策展"其实也不可定义，或者说策展就是对于策展本身的不断定义，它不仅是艺术与社会运动的一部分，其本身也是一种运动。

当然，从执行和实施的角度讲，策展还是有自己的一套基本规范（详见《策展人手册》《独立策展人》等相关书籍）——尽管这套规范不见得适用于所有的机构和策展人。归根结底，我觉得策展还是一种经验，靠的还是积累。

不过我更关心的问题是，我们为什么要策展？或者说，策展人的工作与艺术写作、学术研究的区别是什么？除了作为一种职业，到底是什么动力促使我们选择这样一个行业？它的不可替代性在哪里？

事实上这也是长期困扰我的一个问题。同样，这也是一个没有标准答案的问题，每个人的际遇和理解都不一样。对于你们来说，大多数人一开始可能学的就是这个专业和方向，都受过系统的教育和训练，所以它一开始就是一种职业选择。而我们这一代或更老的一代中国策展人中的大多数在进入这个行业之初，对于策展本身并没有一个清晰的认识和系统的理解，而是在某个时机被卷进来的。比如我自己，最早是尝试写一些评论，很晚才开始接触策展。这个转变的过程也没有系统地接受过相关的专业培训，基本靠自己摸索和学习。最初看的展览少，视野有限，所以理解得很简单。后来慢慢地有了自己的判断和想法，特别是对于现场以及策展的不可替代性，有了更深的体会。越往后就越觉得策展是理论思考和学术写作无法替代的。我们固然可以把展览换成写作，但很多时候，它可能比后者更具感知力和政治性。我之前和2019青策计划获选策展人王欢交流的时候也说过，由于展览的逻辑性通常没有文章那么缜密，反而更具开放性和丰富的层次。有一些其他方式和途径（比如写作）传递不了的感受和想法，展览可以实现。经过这些年的实践和历练，"为什么要策展"这个问题，逐渐变得越来越清晰和明确。

如果从策展史的角度讲，一个重要的变化是上世纪90年代初全球化时代的来临，特别是1997年的卡塞尔文献展，被视为世纪之交的"文化宣言"。若按照柄谷行人的说法，全球化带来的一个重要的变化是："结构"转向了"事件"。简单地说，在这之前，无论是形式主义，还是结构主义或后结构主义，都在诉诸一种

"结构性"的思考和实践，但1990年代以后，一个根本的变化是，"事件"替代了"结构"。譬如近一、二十年当红的那些所谓的知识分子，包括巴迪欧、阿甘本、朗西埃等，特别是齐泽克，他们的写作都带着强烈的事件性。展览也是一样。1990年代以前，大多展览关心的是艺术或艺术史的问题，但这之后，"事件性"成了策展的主要趋向。"事件"往往无法提供结构性的深度思考，所以都是临时的，不确定的，媒体化的，甚至是转瞬即逝的。直到今天，依然如此。在很大程度上，可以说策展就是制造事件，它的政治性也体现在这里。这应该是我们今天策展最主要的动力源头。

如何策展？

前面说到，策展很大程度上靠的是经验，通常每个机构都有自己的属性和基本规范。但到底如何策展，首先有必要对策展这一职业本身作一简单的区分。

其一、艺术史的书写或重构。今天主要是美术馆和艺术机构在做这个类型的展览，通常每个馆和机构都有自己的专业策展人，而且他们都有着明确的分工。最典型的是 MoMA 扩建后的新藏品展，它不仅改变了依据时间、区域或媒介、流派、图式的传统历史叙事，更基于当下最紧迫的文化和政治议题，展开了一部新的全球史叙事。比如将毕加索的《阿维农少女》和费思·林格尔德的《美国人民系列 #20：死亡》并置在一起，类似这样的陈列非常多图示1, P6。这种方法其实并不新鲜，据说20世纪90年代泰特美术馆就已经实验过，但是基于 MoMA 的藏品规模，特别是它的全球视野和精心部署还是让人耳目一新。这样的展览当然是建立在丰富的藏品和足够的经费支持之上，问题是，如果没有藏品或藏品有限，又或者经费不足，怎么办？前几年，克莱尔·毕肖普写过一本小册子《激进美术馆学：当代美术馆的

1.

MoMA 改建后的新藏品展现场，毕加索的《阿维农少女》和费思·林格尔德的《美国人民系列#20：死亡》并置。图片由讲者提供。

Les Demoiselles d'Avignon by Pablo Picasso and *American People Series #20: Die* by Faith Ringgold juxtaposed at the newly overhauled Museum of Modern Art. Image courtesy of the lecturer.

2.

展览"行动剧场：海湾战争 (1991–2011)"，MoMA PS1, 2019年。图片源于 MoMA PS1 官网，由 Matthew Septimus 拍摄。© 2019 MoMA PS1.

"The Gulf Wars 1991–2011", MoMA PS1, 2019. Images from the official website of MoMA PS1. Photo by Matthew Septimus. © 2019 MoMA PS1.

当代性》，讨论了三个案例：西班牙马德里的索菲亚皇后国家艺术中心博物馆、荷兰恩荷芬的凡艾伯当代美术馆及斯洛文尼亚卢布尔雅那的梅特柯瓦当代美术馆，他们是如何应对这个问题的，非常有启发。

除此之外，就是艺术家个展，特别是大型回顾展。比如2018年MoMA举办的安德里安·派普的回顾展，从她20世纪六、七十年代的概念艺术到后来语言、媒介多变的政治性实践，可以清晰地看到一个艺术家的蜕变过程，她一个人就构成了一部艺术史。另一个我印象比较深的是几年前在巴塞尔现代美术馆看过的皮卡比亚的回顾展，那就是一部20世纪上半叶的艺术史。当然，这些展览都是建立在策展人深度研究的基础之上，可能需要策展人和整个策展和研究团队花一两年，甚至更长的时间去准备。

其二，主题性展览。除了全世界的双/三年展、文献展以外，主要是各大美术馆和机构策划的专题性展览，举两个例子，一个是PS1正在展的"行动剧场：海湾战争（1991–2011）"图片2, P7，另一个是2018年大都会博物馆布劳耶分馆举办的"一切皆有关联：艺术与阴谋"。这两个展览的针对性很强，政治性很明确，"行动剧场"是小型双年展的规模，看似是在反思这段历史，但它针对的则是今天依然非常复杂的中东局势。因为最近美国和伊朗关系的白热化，这个展览的效应还在进一步放大。"一切皆有关联"也是，它回顾了20世纪60年代至2016年特朗普上台之前有关"艺术与阴谋"的艺术实践，他们从中选择了七十余件作品参展，题材几乎涵盖了半个世纪以来发生在美国或涉及美国的那些诡谲而尖锐的政治事件，包括肯尼迪遇刺、水门事件、民权运动、伊拉克战争、"9·11"恐怖袭击、国家监视系统、无人机战争伦理等。但实际上，它针对的是2016年美国总统大选催生的一个新的时代，即所谓的"后真相时代"。

其三，"新艺术"的发现和推动。这种展览通常都是要引领艺术潮流的，最典型的就是新美术馆三年展，他们通常花两三年时间在全球范围去调研，寻找可能代表当下或未来艺术方向的艺术家和作品。所谓新艺术也不见得全是年轻艺术家，还有一些被历史遮蔽的老艺术家，这些年冒出来很多；还有就是一些所谓的"非当代艺术"的实践进入当代艺术系统，比如我2019看的展览里有几个关于音乐的反而印象很深，马德里 CaixaForum 文化中心的"歌剧：激情、力量与政治"图示3, P10，惠特尼美术馆的杰森·莫兰个展等。除了美术馆以外，这里值得一提的是那些中小型画廊，其实在"新艺术"的发现和推动上也扮演着非常重要的角色，它们发现了很多艺术家，尽管很多可能后来都被大画廊和超级画廊挖走了，但这些小画廊主的"触角"其实非常敏锐。20世纪六七十年代纽约的那些激进的新前卫实验大多都是由保拉·库珀画廊这样的画廊支持的。2018年夏天巴德学院黑塞美术馆举办过一个展览"艺术存在的条件"，回顾了帕特·赫恩画廊和美国艺术公司的历史，这个展览当时备受好评，它虽是一个特殊的案例和样本，但从中可以看到1983至2004这二十年间，纽约下城区鲜活的艺术生态。图示4, P11

其四，非营利艺术机构和独立空间的展览。这些机构通常都有自己明确的方向，比如纽约的 The Kitchen 主要是做表演的，Sculpture Center 主要针对的是雕塑。它们一方面致力于表演或雕塑媒介语言的实验和拓展，但同时也通过展览发出它们的独立声音。当然也有综合性的，比如伦敦的海沃美术馆、ICA，米兰的普拉达基金会这样的机构，它们其实都是小型美术馆，展览质量都非常高。

其五，其他。比如各种临时空间的临时展览，这种展览更灵活，也更具不确定性，有的展览可能开幕完就结束了，它就像一个运动和事件，对策展人的能力是一种考验。20世纪90年代国内

3.

"歌剧：激情、力量与政治"的
展览海报及展览现场，图片源自
马德里 CaixaForum 文化中心官
网。© CaixaForum

Poster and installation view of the
exhibition, "Opera: Passion, Power and
Politics". Images from the official website
of CaixaForum Madrid. © CaixaForum

4.

"艺术存在的条件"展览现场，
图片源自黑塞美术馆官网。
© Hessel Museum of Art

Installation view of "The Conditions of
Being Art". Image from the website of
Hessel Museum of Art. © Hessel Museum
of Art

5.

"疆域：地缘的拓扑"展览现场，
2017年。图片由讲者提供。

Installation view of the exhibition,
"Frontier: Reassessment of Post-
Globalisation Politics", 2017. Image
courtesy of the lecturer.

的大多展览都是这样的，而且大部分都是艺术家策划的，这一点翁子健的讲座应该已经详细讲过了，我就不重复了。

展览其实有很多种，以上所列举的这些并不能涵盖所有，而且，我们应该警惕这种分类，策展的目的之一也是希望从这种僵化的区分中跳脱出来。

策展人如何在不同的机构里付诸实践

下面我想简单介绍三个我自己的展览。其实我不大喜欢介绍自己的工作，而且我觉得展览就是用来现场体验的，这里就不详细展开来谈，快速地过一遍，感兴趣的朋友可以上网搜一些相关的资料看。

第一个展览是"疆域：地缘的拓扑"图示5，P12，2017年底在 OCAT 上海馆举办，2018年3月结束后巡展到 OCAT 研究中心（北京馆）。它算是我第一个真正想做的，而且完全实现了的展览。这个展览不太一样的是，在展览之前，我已经完成了论文的初稿，展览的主题、框架都是根据文章的结构建立的，艺术家名单也基本上是在文章里提到的。这个展览的特点就是主题高度明确，作品都是围绕着主题选择的。为什么选择这个主题？我们知道，2016年以来随着全球地缘政治的变化，民族、宗教、疆界等问题变得更加突出也更加复杂，一度成为了世界性的热点话题。这期间我也一直在留意这些讨论，阅读一些相关的著述。所以在2017年初的时候，我就想从艺术的角度作一些思考。最初只是想写一篇文章，后来张培力老师找我策划一个展览，当下就决定把它实现，他听了以后二话没说就通过了。整个展览执行的过程也非常顺畅，团队非常专业。

因为是从论文转换过来的，所以展览有着清晰的结构和线索，

6.

"在集结"展览现场，沈阳 K11艺术中心，2018年。图片由讲者提供。

Installation view of the exhibition, "Assembling", Shenyang K11 Art Mall, 2018. Image courtesy of the lecturer.

从引言"长城叙事"到第一单元"民族—国家与边界"、第二单元"民族、宗教与边疆"、第三单元"后全球化时代的移动与身份"，直至尾声"未来的疆界"，层层递进。从蔡国强《万里长城延长一万米》开始，到赵汀阳的一张漫画《我的边疆》结束。艺术家和参展作品的选择上，有老作品，也有最新的创作，除了大陆艺术家，还有不少港台艺术家，我希望还是将问题复杂化，而不仅仅是传递一种信息和态度。现场我希望传递一种动荡感，所以第一次很大胆地使用了一些之前没用过的方式。还组织了十几场学术研讨和对话，20余位国内著名的学者应邀参与。应该说，这是迄今我做过的最重要的一个展览。

第二个展览是"在集结"图示6，P14。这个展览是沈阳 K11 艺术中心的开馆展，是由我和张涵露共同策划的，我负责主题馆部分，她负责城市项目。相比而言，这个展览的难度比较大，首先它是一个命题作文，必须围绕东北这个区域，所有参展艺术家都是东北的或跟东北有关的。其次是在我介入之前，他们已经做了一些调研和初步的计划，基本方向已经确定。关键是，我对东北和东北艺术完全不熟悉。因此对我来说，这是一次不小的挑战。展览的初衷就是希望为一直以来萎靡不振的东北经济、文化和艺术注入一种新的能量。当然，我们知道从1980年代起，东北是一个重要的文化和艺术区域，历史上有一些非常重要的绘画作品，都来自鲁迅美术学院，到了1990年代，又涌现了一批优秀的纪录片、摄影和地下音乐作品，所以当年东北的艺术生态是非常活跃和前卫的，但后来随着东北地区经济优势的转移，文化、艺术也沉了下去。所以我们选择了"在集结"这个主题，希望重新唤起这些力量。英文"Assembling"来自哈特和奈格里的新书《Assembly》，两位作者提出了如何通过横向运动激发政治战略和决策能力，以实现持久的民主变革。援引至此，是希望将这种政治性带到这个展览里。

7.

"没有航标的河流，1979"展览
现场，2019年。图片
由讲者提供。

Installation view of the exhibition, "On a
River Without Navigation Marks, 1979",
2019. Image courtesy of the lecturer.

在设计展览结构的时候，我希望把东北特有的幽默感和区域文化传递出来，采用了一些非常有趣的题目，它们都来自参展艺术家的作品标题：《姐夫再忙，也没有忘记你……》《过去的情人变老了》《不知你走了多久，也不知你要去什么地方》《当看不再是一种选择》《一场革命还未来得及定义》。串联起来像一首诗，可又不是一首严格意义上的诗，不过能感觉到某种情绪在里面。展览的最后一个单元叫作《起始：一场革命还未来得及定义》，以1980年代东北的三个艺术小组结束：紫罗兰油画研究会、北方艺术群体和北方道路艺术联盟。展览展出了他们以前的作品以及相关的文献档案。之所以以他们作为结尾，也是希望成为一个新的起点。值得一提的是那些老艺术家，有的已经80多岁了，他们一开始都不愿意借作品给我们，因为他们以前借出去的作品很多都没拿回来。直到开幕时看了展览，他们非常感动，觉得我们非常专业。

第三个展览是"没有航标的河流，1979" 图示7，P16，这是2019年9月在博而励画廊举办的一个展览，有50多个艺术家参展。和前面两个展览不一样，这个展览是画廊主办的，自然就会涉及到作品的销售，所以会有一些这方面的限制和阻力。也就是说，选择艺术家的时候必须优先考虑画廊自己的艺术家。也因为是画廊的展览，个别艺术家拒绝参加这个展览。所以在这种条件下，怎么样把展览做出来，而且还能充分表达主题，对我是一个不小的挑战。画廊非常重视这个展览，我大概前后提交了三次方案，最后选择了目前这个方案，一方面是可操作性比较强，另一方面是可以兼顾到画廊的一些基本要求。

展览虽然是从1979年的"星星美展"谈起，但实际上，它是一部围绕1979年的大叙事，涵盖了中国改革开放四十年的历史。但有一个主线是我想传递的：这四十年来，到底是什么形塑了我们的价值观和世界观。展览标题"没有航标的河流，1979"来自叶

8.

"街角、广场与蒙太奇"展览现	Installation view of the exhibition,
场,2019年。图片由讲者提供。	"Corner, Square and Montage", 2019.
	Image courtesy of the lecturer.

蔚林1980年的中篇小说《在没有航标的河流上》，1983年，导演吴天明将它改编成电影《没有航标的河流》。小说和电影虽然是反思文革的，但它们的叙事方式很意识流，很接近我们关于改革开放这四十年的基本感觉。展览除了艺术家作品以外，我还动用了很多文本文献、视频和音频档案，整体更像是那个年代的一个视觉文化展，我希望通过这些元素把那个时代感带出来。展览的三个部分"圆明园""形式美"和"可口可乐"，"圆明园"是把1979年改革开放的大语境带出来，包括"中美建交""伊朗革命"等，同时追溯到"火烧圆明园"这一历史事件，并引申出1995年圆明园画家村的历史。关于"形式美"和"可口可乐"，我是作为一种意识形态来梳理的。可以看出，整个展览的思路其实非常明确。展览的结尾是"ONS艺术小组"，这是一个刚刚成立不久的临时的、松散的绘画小组，以回应1979年的"星星美展"和"无名画会"。我的一个基本感觉是："ONS"虽然不具有诸如"星星""无名"那样的革命性和转折意义，但其提醒我们，我们又到了一个新的历史关头。而体现在他们身上的迷茫和无力感，或许正是这个时代最恰切的表征。

前段时间我完成了展览画册的文章，写了三万多字。写文章的时候发现自己最初的一些感觉是有问题的。不像"疆域：地缘的拓扑"，先是写了文章，展览完全是按文章去布置的。而"没有航标的河流，1979"开始是凭感觉去找作品、组织展览结构，最后再去写作，可以看出展览和写作各自自足的一面及其差异所在。

除了这三个展览，最近策划的"街角、广场与蒙太奇"（武汉）图示8，P18、"不可抗力"（纽约）这两个小展览，也是我比较看重的。虽然展览不大，但同样体现了当下我最真实的体认和态度。前者是关于革命的展览，我把它追溯到爱森斯坦的《十月》，联系到美国《十月》杂志，串出唐小禾的《十月》与中国革命，以及当下的一些敏感事件的关系。后者是关于人的有限性和无限欲望的展览，涉及到自然、权力、制度、欲望等。限于时间，这里就不详说了。我想重申的一点是，作为一种政治行动，策展就是要一往无前，不断地制造事件和话题。策展人虽然不是预言家，但可以通过展览，延迟某个特殊的政治时刻，进而批判性地卷入其中。今天，我们的言论空间决定了我们发声的限度，但也因此，兴许反而更能激发我们的能动性和政治力。这当然需要争取和必要的策略，很多时候还不得不妥协，但更重要的是，我们如何始终保持对这个行业的职业精神和激情。

策展实践也促使我对于艺术史有了新的认识，比如关于李格尔的"艺术意志"（Kunstwollen）、瓦尔堡的"情念程式"（Pathosformel）或"文化意志"（Kulturwollen），它们的重心其实不在于提供某种分析模式，而是在于其中的内驱力和能动性。这些理论诞生于一战前后这一特殊的历史时期。百年后，在这一同样交织着理性与疯狂的新历史关头，重识这两个概念及其强烈的现实感也逼迫我们重新思考：此时此刻，艺术何为？艺术史何为？面对这些问题，文字的力量是有限的，可能还需要更多展览来回应。

国内的艺术生态想必在座的各位都比较了解，大部分美术馆因为不设专业的策展职位和团队，所以独立策展人很多时候只能服务于画廊。但我觉得国内画廊很了不起，承担了一部分美术馆的功能，也给了策展人很多机会。我相信，未来会逐渐变好的。老话说，"机会永远是留给有准备的人"，所以大家可以平时多积累一些方案，有机会就上。谢谢大家！　　　　　　　■

What is curating? Why do we curate? What are the requirements of curating as a profession? How to perceive the relationship among curating, artistic writing and academic research? What is the biggest obstacle for curating at the moment? Where is the way out for independent curating? ...

Curating is not a new profession. In this particular era of art, curators are faced with unprecedented pressures, challenges as well as opportunities. How does a curator respond to this new change, while maintaining enthusiasm and passion for this profession? With these questions in mind, this lecture centered around a number of recent exhibitions of significance from home and abroad (including some of which curated by the lecturer) and tried to discuss related issues.

Lu Mingjun: Curating, Initiative and Political Power

I would like to thank PSA for its invitation, and would also like to thank Professor Shen Yubing and Dr. Shen Qilan. I'm glad to have this opportunity to share with you my understanding of and experience in curating. Curating is different from theoretical thinking or academic research, because great curation does not come with age, and sometimes the situation might be just the opposite. The younger the sharper, the more motivated you are. Therefore, I'm actually here to communicate with you with a mindset of learning.

Why do we curate?

First, I want to start with a fundamental question, i.e. what is curating? I believe everyone here has your own definition and understanding. It is not difficult for us to find various explanations in relevant professional books. Nevertheless, from my own understanding, similar to the word "contemporary", curating is indefinable as well. In other words, curating is a constant process of self-definition. Curating is not only a part of art and social movement, but also a movement itself. Certainly, from the perspective of execution and implementation, curating still has its own set of basic specifications (see books such as *Curator's Handbook* and *Independent Curators*) even though such specifications may not be applicable to all institutions or curators. After all, curating is also about experience, and requires accumulation.

Nevertheless, I am more interested in the question, why do we curate? In other words, how different is a curator's work from artistic writing or academic research? Apart from being a profession, what motivates us to enter such an industry? What is so irreplaceable about it?

It is a question that has troubled me for a long time, and a question that has no standard answer. Everyone has his/her unique life experience and understanding towards it. For most of you, curating may be a major, a research interest, and a career choice from the beginning, which means you have received systematic education and training. In comparison, most Chinese curators of my generation or older generations first entered the industry without a clear and systematic understanding of curating. We were swept into it at a certain point. In my case, I started earlier with writing art reviews, and began engaged in curatorial practices very late. During the transition, I did not systematically receive any professional training, but explored and learned about curating basically by myself. At first I saw few exhibitions and had limited vision, so I had a brief understanding of curating. Later on, I had my own judgment and ideas, especially on the irreplaceability of the installation view and the curation, which gave me a deeper understanding. As time goes by, I'm increasingly convinced that curating will not be replaced by theoretical thinking or academic writing. Exhibitions may be replaced with writing, but in many cases, they are more perceptible and political than the latter. I once talked with Wang Huan and I said that exhibitions are usually not as logically meticulous as articles, but they have dimensions that are more open and richer. Some perceptions and ideas that cannot be conveyed through other ways and means, such as writing, can be actualized by exhibitions. After years of practice and experience, I find that the answer to the question, "why do we curate", has become clearer in my mind.

From the historical perspective of curating, a major change took place with the advent of globalization in the early 1990s. In particular, Documenta X in Kassel in 1997 is regarded as the "Cultural Declaration" at the turn of the century. According to Kojin Karatani, a major change brought about by globalization is that "structure" has been overtaken by "events". In brief, before the change, be it formalism, structuralism or post-structuralism, they all turned to "structural" thinking and practice. However, since the 1990s, a fundamental change is that "structure" has been replaced by "events". For example, the polular intellectuals in the past decade or two including Alain Badiou, Giorgio Agamben, Jacques Rancière and especially Slavoj Žižek, their writings all strongly possess the nature of "events". It is the same story with exhibitions. Prior to the 1990s, most exhibitions focused on art or art history, but after the 1990s, "events" became the primary trend of curatorial practice. "Events" often cannot provide structural deep thinking; they are temporary, uncertain, mediatized and even fleeting, which remains so today. To a large extent, curating is the making of events, so to speak, which also reflects its political nature. This should be the main source of motivation for curating nowadays.

How to curate?

As mentioned earlier, curating to a large extent relies on experience, and almost each institution has its own attributes and basic norms. Nevertheless, when it comes to how to curate, it is necessary to first make a distinction between the segments of this profession.

First, exhibitions about the writing or reconstruction of art history, which are mostly done by art museums and institutions today. Generally, each museum or institution has its own professional curators with roles and responsibilities clearly set. A typical example is the latest exhibition of collection of the overhauled Museum of Modern Art (MoMA). It has abandoned the traditional approach of a historical narrative based on time and region, or media, genre and schema, and expanded a new narrative from the perspective of global history embracing the most pressing cultural and political issues at the moment. For example, *Les Demoiselles d'Avignon* by Pablo Picasso and *American People Series #20: Die* by Faith Ringgold are juxtaposed in the gallery [Fig. 1, P6]. Although there are many other similar display methods and the juxtaposition is nothing new——it is said that the Tate Museum has experimented about such display methods in the 1990s. Considering the scale of MoMA's collection, especially its global vision and careful deployment, all these efforts make the exhibition refreshing. No doubt that such exhibition depends on a rich collection and sufficient funding. The question is, what if there is no or only limited collection, or insufficient funding? A few years ago, Claire Bishop wrote a pamphlet called *Radical Museology: Or What's Contemporary in Museums of Contemporary Art?*, where she looks into three cases, i.e. Museo Nacional Centro de Arte Reina Sofía in Madrid, Spain, Van Abbemuseum in Eindhoven, Netherlands, and Museum of Contemporary Art (MSUM) in Ljubljana, Slovenia, and how they respond to this question. It is very enlightening.

In addition, artists' solo exhibitions, especially large-scale retrospectives. For example, Adrian Piper's retrospective exhibition held by MoMA in 2018 featured from her conceptual art in the 1960s and 1970s, to her political practice of changing language and media, which gave a clear idea how the artist transformed— she herself has constituted an art history. Another impressive one for me is the retrospective of Francis Picabia, which I saw at the Museum of Contemporary Art Basel a few years ago. It is an art history of the first half of the 20th century. These exhibitions are based on curators' in-depth researches, and may take the curators and the entire curating and research team one or two years, if not longer, to prepare.

Second, thematic exhibitions. Next to the biennial/ triennial and documentary exhibitions around the world, we have thematic exhibitions curated by major art museums and institutions. Here are two examples. One is the "Theater of Operations: The Gulf Wars 1991–2011" currently on show at PS1 [Fig. 2, P7], and the other is "Everything is Connected: Art and Conspiracy" held by the Met Breuer in 2018. The two exhibitions are highly targeted and politically explicit. The "Theater of Operations" with the scale of a small biennale, seems to reflect on the history of the Gulf Wars, but actually points to the current situation in the Middle East, which is still very complex today. The influence of this exhibition is being further magnified due to rising tensions between the United States and Iran. So is "Everything Is Connected", which reviews more than 70 works on art and conspiracy from the 1960s to 2016 before Trump took office, and features spooky and sharp political events over the past half-century in the United States or involving the United States, including the assassination of Kennedy, the Watergate scandal, the African-American Civil Rights Movement, the Iraq War, the September 11 terrorist attacks, the national surveillance system, and Drones and the Ethics of War. In fact, it targets at a new era created by the 2016 US election, the so-called "post-truth era".

Third, the discovery and promotion of "new art". Exhibitions that fall into this category often lead the artistic trend. The most representative one is the New Museum Triennial. Curators spend two or three years on research around the world to find artists and works that may represent the direction of current or future art. Though called new art, it is not necessarily only about young artists. Some elder artists who were obscured in history are coming into view over the years. Besides, so-called "non-contemporary arts" practices have entered the contemporary art landscape, for example, I've seen several impressive exhibitions on music like "Opera. Passion, Power and Politics" at CaixaForum Madrid [Fig. 3, P10], Janson Moran's solo exhibition at the Whitney Museum, etc. Apart from art museums, small and medium-sized galleries are also worth noting, because they also play a vital role in discovering and promoting "new art", and have discovered many artists. Although many of the artists may be later poached by large and mega galleries, the "tentacles" of these small gallery owners are very acute. Those radical avant-garde experiments happened in New York City in the 1960s and 1970s, were mostly supported by galleries like Paula Cooper Gallery. In the summer of 2018, the Hessel Museum of Art, CCS Galleries hosted an exhibition, "The Conditions of Being Art", revisiting the history of Pat Hearn Gallery and American Fine Arts, Co., which was highly praised at the time. It is a special case and specimen, but from which we can see the lively art ecology in New York City over the 20 years from 1983 to 2004. [Fig. 4, P11]

Fourth, exhibitions by non-profit art institutions and independent spaces. These institutions often have their own clear direction, e.g. The Kitchen in New York City focuses on performance, and SculptureCenter highlights sculpture. They are committed to the experiment and expansion of the media language of performance or sculpture, and at the same time, are expressing their independent voice through exhibitions. In addition, there are comprehensive institutions, such as Hayward Gallery and Institute of Contemporary Arts (ICA) in London, and Prada Foundation in Milan, all of which are small in size, but make exhibitions in high quality.

Fifth, others, such as temporary exhibitions in various temporary spaces. Such exhibitions are more flexible and more uncertain—some may end right after opening, like a movement and event, challenging curators' capabilities. Most of the exhibitions in China in the 1990s were like this, and most of them were organized by artists. Anthony Yung has given a detailed introduction about this history in his lecture, so I won't repeat it here.

There are many kinds of exhibitions, and what listed above does not cover all. Moreover, we should be wary of such classification, because one purpose of curating is to escape from this rigid distinction.

How curators do practice at different institutions?

I would like to briefly introduce three exhibitions I curated. In fact, I don't quite like introducing my work, because I think exhibitions are for on-site experience. I will not go into details but go over them quickly. Those who are interested can look them up on the Internet.

The first exhibition is "Frontier: Re-assessment of Post-Globalisational Politics", held at the OCAT Shanghai in late 2017, and toured in the OCAT Institute (Beijing) after March 2018. It was the first exhibition that I ever wanted to curate and that was fully actualized. This exhibition is unique, because I had completed the first draft of my thesis before the exhibition. The theme and framework of the exhibition were built upon the thesis structure, and the artist list was pretty much the same from the one included in the thesis. The exhibition is characterized by its clear theme, around which the works were selected. Why did I choose this theme? It is known that with the global geopolitical changes since 2016, issues concerning ethnicity, religion and borders have become more prominent and more complex, and once became an international hot topic. During that period, I paid attention to discussions and writings on these issues. In early 2017, I intended to make some critical thinking from an artistic perspective. At first, I just wanted to write an essay, while later Mr. Zhang Peili asked me to curate an exhibition. I immediately decided to do it. Mr. Zhang approved my idea right away after listening to it. The implementation throughout the exhibition was very smooth and the team was very professional.

Developed from a thesis, this exhibition has a clear structure and progressive clues from the introduction "Great Wall Narrative", to the first section "Nation-State and Borders", to the second section "Nations, Religions and Borders", to the third section "Movement and Identity in the Post-Globalization Era", and to the conclusion "Future Frontier". It starts with *Extend the Great Wall of China by 10,000 Meters* by Cai Guoqiang, and ends with the comic *My Frontier* by Zhao Tingyang. When it comes to the selection of artists and works, I featured both old and latest works by artists from the mainland as well as from Hong Kong and Taiwan. I aimed at complicating the issue, and going beyond message and attitude delivery. In the exhibition room, I wanted to convey a sense of turbulence, thus for the first time, I boldly employed some methods that had not been used before. I also organized a dozen academic seminars and conversations, with more than 20 renowned domestic scholars invited. It is fair to say that this is the most important exhibition I have ever curated. Fig. 5, P12

The second exhibition is "Assembling", the inaugural exhibition of Shenyang K11 Art Mall. It was co-curated by me and Zhang Hanlu. I was in charge of the theme pavilion, while she worked on city projects. Relatively speaking, this exhibition was more difficult. First, there was a given theme, i.e. Northeast China. All participating artists should be from or related to Northeast China. Second, the curatorial team already did some research and preliminary plans before I joined them, and the general direction had been determined. The question is, I was completely new to the northeast region and its art. Therefore, it was a big challenge for me. The original intention of the exhibition was to rejuvenate the sluggish economy, culture and art in Northeast China. Obviously, we know that from the 1980s, Northeast China was an important area of culture and art, and a few very important paintings in history are from Lu Xun Academy of Fine Arts. In the 1990s, a number of excellent documentaries, photography and underground music works sprang up. This suggests the art ecology of Northeast China was very active and avant-garde. However, later, as the economic advantages were shifted out of the region, culture and art also sank. That's why we chose the theme of "Assembling" in the hope to restore these strengths. The English name "Assembling" derives from the new book by Michael Hardt and Antonio Negri, *Assembly*. The two authors propose how to stimulate political strategy and decision-making capabilities through horizontal movements to achieve lasting democratic change. To this end, I hope to bring such political properties into this exhibition.

When designing the exhibition structure, I wanted to convey the unique sense of humor and regional culture of the northeast region with some very interesting topics, all of which come from the work titles of the participating artists, i.e. *No Matter How Busy He is, Brother-in-law Won't Forget You...*, *Former Lovers Have All Grown Old*, *Not Sure How Long You've Been Away, or Where You're Going*, *If Seeing Is Not an Option*, and *Some Actions, Which Haven't Been Defined yet in the Revolution*. The exhibition is strung together like a poem. It is not a poem in the strict sense, yet you can sense some emotion in it. The final section is called Overture: Some Actions, Which Haven't Been Defined yet in the Revolution, ending with three art groups from Northeast China in the 1980s, i.e. Violet Oil Painting Research

Association, Northern Art Group, and Northern Road Art Union. The exhibition showcases their previous works and related archives. The exhibition concluded with these groups in the hope to become a new starting point. It is worth mentioning that those old artists, some of which were over 80 years old, were reluctant to lend their works to us at first, because many of the works they had lent were never returned. Yet they were deeply moved and impressed by the professionalism when they saw the exhibition on the opening day of Shenyang K11 Art Center. Fig. 6, P14

The third exhibition is "River floating without a Beacon, 1979", held at the Boers-Li Gallery in September 2019, with more than 50 artists participating. Unlike the previous two exhibitions, this exhibition was hosted by the gallery, thus it would naturally involve the sale of works as a matter of factor and bring restrictions and resistance to the curator in this regard. In other words, when choosing an artist, the priority must be given to artists signed by the gallery. Also, because it is a gallery exhibition, several artists refused to participate. Under such conditions, how to actualize the exhibition and fully express the theme? It was a great challenge to me. The gallery attached great importance to this exhibition, and finally chose the current plan out of the three proposals I submitted, because it is workable and up to basic requirements of the gallery.

Although the exhibition started with the "Star Art Exhibition" in 1979, it is a grand narrative around the year of 1979, covering the 40 years history of reform and opening up in China. The main thread, i.e. what I want to convey, is what has shaped our values and worldview in the past 40 years. The exhibition title "River Floating Without a Beacon, 1979" comes from the novel by Ye Weilin in 1980, *On a River Without Buoys*. In 1983, director Wu Tianming adapted it into a movie, *The River Without Buoys*. Although the novel and the movie reflect on the Cultural Revolution, they both use a stream-of-consciousness narration, which is very close to our primary feelings about the 40 years of reform and opening up. In addition to artists' works, I also employed a number of text documents, videos and audio files, so the exhibition looks more like an exhibition about visual culture of that era. I hope to bring out the sense of that era through these elements. The exhibition consists of three parts, i.e. "Yuanming Yuan" (the Old Summer Palace), "Formal Beauty" and "Coca-Cola". "Yuanming Yuan" unrolls the context of the reform and opening up in 1979, including "the Establishment of China-US Diplomatic Relations" and "Iranian Revolution", and traces back to the historical event, the Burning of Old Summer Palace, and then the history of the Yuanming Yuan Painters' Village in 1995. The section of "Formal Beauty" and "Coca-Cola" are combed through as a perspective of ideology, respectively. As you can see, the thread of the entire exhibition is very clear. The exhibition ends with the ONS Art Group, which is a temporary, loosely organized painters' group that was newly set up in response to the Star Art Exhibition and No Name Painting Society in 1979. I have an essential feeling that although ONS does not have the revolutionary and transformative significance of the Star Art Exhibition and the No Name Painting Society, it reminds us that we have reached a new historical juncture. The confusion and powerlessness we see from ONS may be the most appropriate characterization of this era. Fig. 7, P16

Some time ago, I finished an article of about 30,000 words for the exhibition catalog. When writing the article, I noticed that some of my initial feelings were problematic. Unlike "Frontier: Reassessment of Post-Globalisation Politics", which was completely arranged according to the thesis that had been written, I searched for works and built the exhibition structure based on my intuition, before I finally went for writing when I curated "On A River Without Navigation Marks, 1979". It can be seen that the self-sufficient aspects of exhibition and writing, and as well as their differences from one another.

In addition to these three exhibitions, the two exhibitions I recently curated, "Corner, Square and Montage" in Wuhan Fig. 8, P18 and "Force Majeure" in New York, are also important to me. Although they are not large exhibitions, they have embodied my most authentic cognition and attitude at the moment. "Corner, Square and Montage" is about revolutions. I traced it back to the movie *October* by Sergei Eisenstein, associated it with the American magazine *October* and led to the painting *1976—China's October* by Tang Xiaohe and the revolution in China, as well as several sensitive events of the moment. "Force Majeure" is an exhibition of human finiteness and infinite desires, which involves nature, power, institutions, desires, and so on. Due to time constraints, I won't go into details here. I would like to reiterate that, as a political action, curating is about pressing ahead and continuously creating events and topics. Although a curator is not a prophet, he or she can use the exhibition to extend a particular political moment and get involved critically. Today, the limits on the freedom of speech determine the range of our voice, but this may actually inspire our self-motivation and political initiative. This of course takes efforts and necessary strategies, and at many times, compromises. However, what's more important is how we always maintain the professionalism and passion for this industry.

Curatorial practice has also led me to a new understanding of art history, such as Alois Riegl's Kunstwollen, and Aby Warburg's Pathosformel or Kulturwollen, the significance of which is not about a mode of analysis, but the internal drive and motivation they provide. These theories were proposed in a particular historical period around World War I. A hundred years later, at this new historical juncture, where reason and madness intersect once again, revisiting these two concepts and their strong sense of reality makes us rethink: at this moment, what is art? What is art history? To get back to these questions, as word is not powerful enough, it may take more exhibitions.

Everyone here familiar with the domestic art ecology knows that most art museums do not have professional curatorial positions or teams, thus independent curators often can only work for galleries. However, I think domestic galleries are amazing, as they have taken on some of the functions of museums, giving independent curators plenty of opportunities. I believe that it will get better in the future over time. As the old saying goes, "Chance favors only the prepared mind", you can accumulate more curatorial plans and seize the opportunity when there is one. Thank you.   ∎

青策充电站
联合主办：上海当代艺术博物馆、复旦大学哲学学院

工作团队
上海当代艺术博物馆：张琍莉、马慧婷、徐辰斐、邱鼎、黄彦娜
复旦大学哲学学院：袁新、林晖、沈奇岚、陈佳

实录册编辑团队
编辑：马慧婷、蔺佳
平面设计：邵君瑜
翻译：曾晨
校对：阮汇善

ECP Charging Station Programme
Co-organizers: Power Station of Art,
School of Philosophy, Fudan University

Programme Team
Power Station of Art: Zhang Lili, Ma Huiting, Xu Chenfei,
Qiu Ding, Huang Yanna
School of Philosophy, Fudan University: Yuan Xin, Lin Hui,
Shen Qilan, Chen Jia

Editorial Team
Editor: Ma Huiting, Lin Jia
Graphic Design: Shao Junyu
Translator: Zen Chen
Proofreader: Ruan Huishan

青策充电站
策展与艺术哲学
工作坊

实录

ECP Charging
Station
Workshop Series:
Curating and
Philosophy of Art

Record

本课讲座旨在勾勒从罗杰·弗莱，到格林伯格、施坦伯格、夏皮罗的英美现代艺术的伟大批评传统。这一传统通常被认为是仅次于法国从18世纪中叶狄德罗到19世纪中叶的波德莱尔的那个批评传统。讲座结合这一英美艺术批评写作史上的经典作品，分析了不起的批评写作应当是怎样的，以及这样的批评在当代艺术条件下遇到了什么样的困境，最后讨论艺术批评突围的可能性及其方式。

沈语冰：艺术批评写作的伟大传统及其危机

艺术批评传统的悠久历史

策展和批评这两方面，我认为严格来讲不能完全分开。因为也许艺术批评最晚期的形态已经变成了策展，以策展的方式挑选艺术家、呈现艺术批评的视野，这本身就需要一种批评家的眼光。

当然艺术批评还能够为策展提供养分。因为相较于有悠久历史的艺术批评传统，策展是一个相对晚近的新生事物。大家如果去看文杜里写的《西方艺术批评史》，他是从古代希腊和罗马开始写起。如果写中国的艺术批评史，我们也可以上溯到先秦两汉，那时就有一些零星的思想片断、关于批评的某些个案。到了魏晋南北朝时期，围绕文学、诗歌、绘画、书法展开的批评显然已经达到了很高的自觉程度。所以说，大概自从有艺术活动，或者至少当艺术活动进入到一个相对的公共领域开始，就伴随着艺术批评。艺术批评具有悠久的历史和很了不起的传统。

我今天和大家聊的主要侧重于英美在20世纪这100年内建立起来的艺术批评传统，没有谈中国古代的艺术批评——当然这是另外一个非常悠久的、非常了不起的传统。近代艺术批评有两个重心：18至19世纪的法国，以及19世纪下半叶到20世纪下半叶的英美。在谈英美之前，我要稍微谈一下18至19世纪法国的艺术批评。

我大概会讲到罗杰·弗莱、格林伯格、施坦伯格、夏皮罗、迈克尔·弗雷德这几个人，但不是巨细无遗地、逐一地来讲。事先没有阅读过他们的文本的人，在我下面的介绍中，听起来可能会有一些困扰。因此我尽量择选出一些最有典型意义的片断，和大家一起阅读，给大家一个初步的概念：好的批评写作应该是怎样的。

在最后，我会谈到20世纪的下半叶到现如今，批评的传统所面临着的一个巨大的危机——批评似乎再也不像18、19、20世纪那么重要了。一方面它越来越多地被策展人的工作所取代，另外批评也面临着很多的现实问题。在古典艺术至现代艺术时期，艺术家更多的是工匠，而不是知识分子。有一个不成文的规定：艺术家不需要读那么多书。如果一个画家，比如塞尚或毕加索，滔滔不绝地做演讲或者成为一名畅销书作家，那是不可思议的。因为这违背了人们对于"沉默的、动手而不动口的"画家和艺术家的传统定义与想象。

但是，20世纪六、七十年代以后，越来越多的艺术家进入到高校学习，甚至读到艺术硕士、博士。他们拥有大量的阅读储备，在思想和理智上，已然不需要有批评家去帮助他们发声了，艺术家本人已经具有批评家的敏锐和高度的智性。这样一来就面临一个问题：批评还需要吗？这是一个很多人都在提的问题。所以，最后我会把这个问题留给大家讨论。

现代艺术批评的前史：从狄德罗和波德莱尔说起

首先让我们简要地回顾一下18世纪中叶到19世纪中叶法国的艺

术批评，当时的法国艺术是整个欧洲艺术的中心。文艺复兴以后，艺术中心基本上还是在意大利：佛罗伦萨、罗马、威尼斯。17世纪以后，意大利开始慢慢地衰落，艺术中心转移到荷兰阿姆斯特丹。18世纪和19世纪艺术主要是在英国和法国开始繁荣。伴随着艺术的繁荣，很多大哲学家、大诗人介入了艺术和艺术史的研究，艺术批评开始成为一种正式的艺术活动，批评写作也成为一种专门的写作类别。这里面两个很关键的人物就是18世纪中叶的狄德罗[图示1, P6]和19世纪中叶的波德莱尔[图示2, P6]。

我们在讲任何一部批评史的时候，狄德罗和波德莱尔肯定是要作为非常重要的人物来谈的。我待会儿会讲到现在还活跃在艺术史和艺术批评界的一位重量级的人物迈克尔·弗雷德，他的主要理论来源可以直接追溯到狄德罗。迈克尔·弗雷德作为史学家和批评家，因为提出"剧场性"这个概念，从而对当代艺术的整个生态产生了巨大的影响。待会儿我要将他作为英美传统里的最后一个人物来重点介绍。

我们都知道，狄德罗是一位百科全书式的学者，是法国启蒙运动的主要干将。他和达朗贝尔主编的《百科全书》在当时引起了巨大的轰动，因为它是对法国乃至整个欧洲的宗教、封建王朝保守势力的一种致命的思想上的打击。启蒙运动开始把教庭和国王这样的世俗权威转移到理性，而理性是谁呢？就是那些参与公共讨论的知识分子。这是由启蒙运动实现的一个转折，而在这个过程当中，狄德罗扮演了一个非常关键的角色。达朗贝尔编了几期以后就退出了，后来只剩下狄德罗一个人在坚持，但是《百科全书》吸引了当时法国乃至欧洲几乎所有主要的知识分子来为它写条目。他们对知识进行重新梳理，和过去神权和王权所建立的知识体系彻底告别，毫无疑问这是一场思想的革命。所以，狄德罗的重要性很关键的一点在于，他是启蒙运动的一个杰出人物。更重要的是，他对艺术批评产生了巨大影

1.

狄德罗画像。除特殊注明外，本文内所有图片由讲者沈语冰提供。

Portrait of Diderot. All photos in this article are courtesy of the speaker Shen Yubing unless otherwise specified.

2.

波德莱尔肖像。

Portrait of Baudelaire.

响：他是第一个为每年在法国沙龙展出的那些绘画进行评论、在报刊上发表评论的人。他作为一个桥梁、一个中介，通过他的艺术批评写作，将官方的展览和订阅报刊的那些城市市民阶层、中产阶级家庭建立起了联系。他的艺术批评写作质量非常高——狄德罗是这样，卢梭和孟德斯鸠都是这样，他们的文本都具有极强的感召力，你读了就心潮澎湃，而不像后来的学院派写作那样四平八稳，讲究证据、逻辑和推理。那个时候的写作者大都是小说家、戏剧家，他们运用小说、戏剧、诗歌的语言和激情来写艺术批评，这也是他们的作品产生深刻影响的一方面原因。一会儿我要讲到艺术批评写作对于语言和文字功底的要求，和这个有关。后面我讲到弗雷德的时候还会回到狄德罗关于批评的主要思想。

到了19世纪中叶，法国就占据了欧洲的思想史和艺术史的主导地位。波德莱尔是19世纪中叶法国最杰出的诗人。而且他巨大的影响力不仅仅在于诗歌，还有很大的一部分是因为他的艺术批评写作。波德莱尔写了一篇非常著名的文章叫《现代生活的画家》，这篇中第一次出现"现代性"这个词，直到21世纪我们还在讨论现代性问题，这都要追溯到19世纪中叶的这位诗人、这位批评家。同时他是第一位把爱伦·坡的诗歌翻译成法文的诗人。近现代了不起的诗人几乎都做过翻译，至少在欧洲的现代诗人里面没有例外，可能中国也一样，比如穆旦。中国民国到后来的大诗人，基本上也都做过翻译，因为他们需要通过翻译来把语言擦亮，通过翻译来了解不同语言之间的差异和相同的地方，从而找到语言的敏锐度。这是很有意思的现象。

波德莱尔最著名的诗集是《恶之花》，他在这里表达了在一个迅速工业化的城市——巴黎——美的那种不断在变化着的本质。他颠覆了过去的传统的经典的美学所讲的，或者学院派所坚持的"美是永恒的"这样一个概念。他认为美是随着时代的变化而变化的。但是他没有在传统派所坚持的美的永恒性，和浪漫派所坚持的美的相对性之间简单地作二元对立，而是很聪明地做了一种调和：他说美的一部分一直在变，一部分是永恒的。我对此的理解是尽管时代在变化，变化的东西很快、很多，但是有些不变的东西也保存着。比如基本的人性是不变的，也许变的是文化对我们的塑造。所以，波德莱尔很巧妙的一点就是说，美这个东西有永恒的一面，也有随着时代的变化而变化的一面。特别是他提出我们从稍纵即逝的现象里提炼出永恒，是一种了不起的能力；而稍纵即逝的各种现象、流动性、变化在他看来就是"现代性"。因为"现代"这个词本来还有一个意思，就是时尚，而变得最快的就是时尚，每一年、每一季都在改变。那么你怎么从时尚里提炼出永恒的、不变的东西呢？这是他提出的核心概念：现代性里面的永恒性——不变的东西和稍纵即逝的东西的辩证。这是很关键的一个思想，我认为不仅仅影响了诗人，还影响了艺术家马奈，并通过马奈影响了整个现代艺术，也就是印象派和后来的现代艺术。某种意义上如果我们一定要去找一种原创性的思想作为现代艺术的发端，这个发端就是波德莱尔。这是我要讲的英美20世纪批评传统的前史，是从狄德罗和波德莱尔开始的。法国有强大的艺术生态，包括艺术生产、展览、消费，然后有最多的艺术评论家。一旦沙龙开幕，法国的报纸连篇累牍都是关于沙龙的某位画家的评论。比如说马奈的《奥林匹亚》展出的时候，巴黎和法国其他的报刊杂志上出现了73篇关于它的评论。现在做一个庞大的双年展也许才会有一定量的报道和批评，如果仅仅围绕一个画家或者他的一幅作品，我们很难想象会有这么多的关注，这么大的影响力。所以，从这样一个简单的数字我们就可以大概琢磨出当时的法国人是多么在乎沙龙展，是多么在乎艺术。现在的法国或许也没有这么大影响力的艺术家。当时的法国给文化保留了一块很大的地盘，后来这个地盘越来越被侵蚀。这是我要讲的18世纪中叶到19世纪中叶法国的艺术批评大致的情况。

罗杰·弗莱：英美现代艺术批评的领军人物

20世纪以后，也是我研究的重点范围，是英美的现代艺术批评。我从罗杰·弗莱开始和大家聊，提纲挈领地勾勒一个大概的轮廓线，我理解的英美现代艺术批评的传统是什么，是怎样的，有哪些主要的领军人物，最后我会概括这些批评大部分都拥有什么样的特征，以及带给我们一些什么样的启示。罗杰·弗莱[图示3，P10]生于19世纪末，在1934年去世，可以说是英美现代艺术史上影响最大的批评家。同时，他也是一位著名的意大利古典绘画鉴定专家，在被任命为美国大都会艺术博物馆的欧洲绘画部主任之前，他已经和美国的伯纳德·贝伦森、意大利的莫雷利并称欧洲古典绘画鉴定的几大权威。但是很有意思的是，弗莱后来更有建树的领域不是古典艺术的鉴定，而是对现代艺术的评论和现代主义美学的奠基。他自己也是一位画家，在剑桥学的是自然科学，后来去法国和意大利学习绘画，然后成为一名意大利绘画的鉴定专家。他自己也不间断地画画，也举办展览。但他在1906年，也就是塞尚去世的那一年，看到塞尚的原作，非常震惊地发现他自己梦寐以求想要画出来的作品，已经有人画出来了。所以弗莱做了一个非常大胆，也是很了不起的决定：放弃了未来成为博物馆馆长的机会，放弃了古典学者的光环，然后为当时在欧洲兴起不久、远没有被一般学者、批评家认可，更不要说被普通公众认可的现代艺术进行辩护。

1910年和1912年罗杰·弗莱在伦敦策划了两次后印象派画展。"Post-Impressionism"（后印象派）这个词就是弗莱杜撰出来的，所以这也是批评家能够进入历史的一个重要原因。早期的现代艺术派别，都是批评家脱口而出的想法，而且很多是贬义的，比如"印象派""野兽派"，都是批评家创造出来骂那些画家的。结果那些印象派画家就用这个名字来展出他们的作品，他们举办了八届画展，从第三届开始使用"印象派"这个词。"后印象

3.

罗杰·弗莱自画像

Roger Fry's Self-Portrait

4.

罗杰·弗莱：《塞尚及其画风的
发展》，沈语冰译，广西师大出
版社，2009；广西美术出版社，
2016

Cézanne: A Study of His Development,
written by Roger Fry and translated by
Shen Yubing, Guangxi Normal University
Press, 2009; Guangxi Fine Arts
Publishing House, 2016

派"是罗杰·弗莱提出来的，用来涵盖塞尚以及塞尚之后的那些画家，以区别于印象派。罗杰·弗莱也是最早的真正意义上既是批评家又是策展人的学者，他跟他的助手克莱夫·贝尔一起跑到欧洲，亲自挑选艺术家和他们的作品。克莱夫·贝尔后来写了一本小书《艺术》，里面提出一个概念叫作"significant form"，我们大多翻译成"有意味的形式"。这是在20世纪八十年代美学界非常流行的一个口号。我们现在很多做美学研究的人，甚至只知道克莱夫·贝尔，却不知道有罗杰·弗莱。实际上克莱夫·贝尔是罗杰·弗莱的助理，而且那本书原来是出版社委托罗杰·弗莱写的，由于罗杰·弗莱对于这种纯理论的书不感兴趣，他就把这个工作交给了他学生辈的克莱夫·贝尔来做。年轻气盛的贝尔一上来就把欧洲的古典美学全部推倒：古典美学是一种题材和主题决定论，而他却认为决定艺术的不是题材、主题，而是形式——艺术是"有意义的形式"（"有意义的形式"是我本人的译法）。他的观点产生了巨大的影响，因此被认为是形式主义美学的一位代表人物。但是实际上他的背后有罗杰·弗莱，以及罗杰·弗莱所在的、以弗吉尼亚·伍尔夫为主的一个伦敦知识分子群体：布卢姆茨伯里派。这是一个很精英的圈子，有小说家、经济学家、诗人、画家、评论家、美学家、哲学家。而弗莱和伍尔夫是这个圈子里的两个重要领袖。弗莱的成就非常之高，后来一位史学家肯尼斯·克拉克，是弗莱在剑桥和牛津的艺术史讲席——斯莱德讲席的接任者。克拉克对罗杰·弗莱有一个著名的评价："罗杰·弗莱是自拉斯金以来对于人们的鉴赏趣味产生了无与伦比的影响的人。如果说趣味可以因为一个人而改变的话，那么这个人就是罗杰·弗莱。"这个评价是最高级的，而且我认为是很中肯的，因为弗莱扭转了拉斯金以来英国公众一般的审美趣味，或者我们所说的品位，使得英国赶上了法国的步伐，不再是一个文化上的孤岛。

罗杰·弗莱主要的一些作品已经翻译成中文，是我们在讲授20

世纪艺术史学史和批评史的时候绕不过去的文献，大家可以了解一下。比如他晚年写的《塞尚及其画风的发展》图示4，P10，弗吉尼亚·伍尔夫认为这是弗莱最伟大的作品。他为后印象派辩护的那些文章，我们都收集在一起，翻译成中文。我提炼出弗莱写作的几个主要特点，不一定很精确，第一个是他的高度的智性和敏锐的感受力。他当然是一位史学家，因为他早年研究意大利的古典艺术，他还是一个画家，同时又接受过自然科学的训练。他是剑桥大学国王学院秘密团体的一员。这个团体每年从国王学院新生里选出一个人，不对外公布，他们会在每周六聚会，每周由一个人围绕一本书来讲他的一个观点，然后遭受所有已毕业的或未毕业的、国王学院选出来的精英的猛烈批评，主讲人再进行答辩，通过这样的训练来达到一种智力的高度。很多年以后人们才知道这个团体里面有哪些人，罗杰·弗莱是其中一个。另一点，他的写作所使用的语言非常精确明晰，意态高华，具有英国绅士的风度。一会儿我跟大家一起来念几段他的评论文字，就会觉得这才是真正的评论家应有的辩论的姿态，不急不躁，用一种很婉约或者很客气的语调，潜移默化地改变了读者的看法。这是很了不起的一种写作方式。最后一个特点就是，我认为他有极强的共情或者移情的能力。比如他在写塞尚的时候，我作为译者经常会有这样的感觉：弗莱这一段是在写塞尚还是在写他自己？他与塞尚作品的共情达到那样的程度，你有时候不知道他是在写塞尚呢，还是在写他自己呢。没有这种共情和感同身受的能力，我认为也写不了一流的评论文章。

大家如果去看弗莱的一些文本就会知道他的文字的优雅以及辩论的高明之处。比如他在反对印象派的模仿论时，是这么说的：

> 后印象派已经开始抛弃印象派的如实再现，或者说如实的模仿，那么人们自然会提出这样的问题，为什么艺术家要这样放纵地抛弃文艺复兴以来赋予人类所有的绘画科学的东西呢？为什么后印象派要任性地回到原始艺术，开始吸收一些非西方的所谓的"原始艺术"的

东西，或者如人们嘲弄的所谓的"野蛮艺术"呢？回答是，这既不是任性也不是放纵，而是出于必然，假如艺术想要从自身的科学方式的不断累积的、毫无希望的臃肿当中解放出来的话，假如艺术想要重新获得表达思想情感的力量，而不是诉诸拜倒在艺术家危险技艺之下的好奇与惊叹的话。

这种回答非常巧妙，他用读者可以接受的一种语言来说理。比如他又说道：

现代艺术已经来到了印象主义，在那里，它能够以前所未有的便捷与精确描绘任何可见的东西，同时也是在那里，在赋予绘画的任何一部分以精确的视觉价值的同时，它在述说被描绘的事物的任何人性意义(human import)时却陷于无能为力的境地。

他认为，印象派在再现的功能上已经达到了几乎和相机一样的精确度，但是在诉说被描绘事物的人性意义的时候，它却无能为力。所以他说：

它并不能从物质上改变事物的视觉价值，因为整体统一于此，而且仅次于此。但是要赋予对大自然的描绘以回应人类激情与人类需求的能力，就要求重估现象，不是根据纯粹的视觉，而是要根据人类理智预定的要求。

除了单纯的视觉以外，它还要遵从人类的理智，就是要与人的知性联系起来，所以这被认为是塞尚的重要贡献：不是仅仅画出眼睛看到的、画出视觉，而是画出了他对视觉所进行的重新调整。这是弗莱另外一本评论文集取名为《视觉与设计》的原因。即赋予视觉以某种设计的结构感。视觉是感性的，而设计具有知性的成分参与其中。所以，罗杰·弗莱用很浅显的语言，几句话就把这个问题讲清楚了。

再比如弗莱对霍利戴先生的回应。霍利戴批评塞尚的《浴者》图示5, P14

5.

塞尚《浴者》(c.1898-1905)，图
片来源于 Google Art Project。
图片来源于大英博物馆官网。
© The Trustees of the British
Museum

The Bather (c.1898-1905), Paul Cézanne.
Photo courtesy of Google Art Project.
Photo credit to the website of the
British Museum. © The Trustees of the
British Museum

6.

拉斐尔《圣母子》素描(c.1506-
1507)，图片来源于大英博物
馆官网。© The Trustees of the
British Museum

Raphael's sketch, *The Virgin and Child*
(c.1506-1507). Photo credit to the
website of the British Museum. © The
Trustees of the British Museum

里面有过多的线条，他认为根据古典绘画的传统应该把线条隐去。弗莱要反驳霍利戴的批评，他说：

> 从这样的一个角度来讲，塞尚的《浴者》完全被他说中了，不过不幸的是，霍利戴先生说得太过了。他所说的一切几乎都适用于拉斐尔《圣母子》图示6，P14素描。要是霍利戴先生想要维持其立场的一贯性，他一定得说谁看见过一个女人的头部，那鹅蛋脸上会有两道三道轮廓线，谁看见过头发底下会露出头盖骨的线条，谁看见过她的脸颊上会有许多平行的黑影线？他必定会提出这样那样的批评。他忘记了艺术利用自然的再现作为表达的手段，但是再现本身却不是目的，因此不能成为批评的准则。

弗莱用四两拨千斤的话语，把对手给打回去了。因为如果你说塞尚画错了，他的人物里面有太多的线条，那么请看拉斐尔画的素描，圣母的脸上有大量平行的影线，你说一个女人的脸上会有那么多黑色的线吗？所以说所有的绘画都只是在媒介和惯例的基础上形成的东西。罗杰·弗莱就这么用轻描淡写的几句话把霍利戴先生给打发了，我认为这是非常厉害的，可能与这位绅士在剑桥国王学院所接受的那种训练有关。

前面属于罗杰·弗莱为后印象派辩护的理论创作，他对塞尚的评论当中，我就引用一段话，我把它分成了四段，其实在原作里面就一段。他在讲到塞尚早期的一幅作品《宴会》图示7，P16，或者也有人称为《醉酒的人》，就是一群喝得酩酊大醉的人，男男女女赤身裸体。塞尚在博物馆里面看到过很多巴洛克绘画，但是他不知道那些画是怎么画出来的。没有人教过他，他只能凭自己的感觉自学，所以从构图到人物造型一塌糊涂。但是罗杰·弗莱说他的色彩是一流的：

> 作品的颜料相当厚重，堆积了不少笔触层次。观众可以看到塞尚那果敢手笔的痕迹，也可以看到为了实现其梦想而付出代价的痛苦努力的痕迹。不管怎么说，他的笔触始终明朗而精致，色彩也始终鲜

7.

塞尚早期作品《宴会》(c.1870)　　Cézanne's early work *The Banquet* (c. 1870)

艳而纯粹。然而，人们却可以从中一窥这一非凡人物的英雄主义，是如何可能以如此不妥协的坦率，如此决绝的确信来制作一份关于现象的最荒诞不经的陈述的。人们也可以认识到他身上一个永远不会背叛他的才能：他那无可挑剔的色彩感。就在他为了获得某种融贯再现，为了某种写实的逼真性而绝望地工作的时候，他的每一笔也从不虚下，不是增加了作品的和谐性，就是为富有创造力的色彩大合唱平添了丰富性。正是在他的色彩中，我们才能发现他那最根本的品质，以及他那种造型创造力的首要灵感来源。色彩感是塞尚身上的一个基本品质，在任何情况下都保持着绝对伟大的水准。此幅也许是他最早的作品宣言，预告了塞尚命中注定要为艺术做出的最伟大贡献之一，那就是，他那种认为色彩不是附丽于形式，也不是强加于形式的东西，而是形式的一个直接组成部分的观念。

所以，虽然弗莱认为塞尚早期的作品，构图失败了，人物造型失败了，但是他的色彩感是一流的。我总觉得面对塞尚作品的时候很激动，但是我们说不出话来，这个时候突然遇到了罗杰·弗莱，他把这些话说出来了。

格林伯格：形式主义美学的集大成者

把罗杰·弗莱的形式主义美学推进到极致的是格林伯格图示8，P18，后现代主义兴起以后，所有火力都对准他开火。格林伯格是非常重要的一个人物，与美国20世纪现代艺术史紧密地联系在一起。他形成了形式主义的美学，当然最有名的是他关于抽象表现主义的观点，以及波洛克和他的个人关系。格林伯格生前唯一出版的自选集是《艺术与文化》图示9，P18。

格林伯格和弗莱有一些共同的地方，比如说都很精确，语言简洁而又明晰；但是他和弗莱又有一些区别，比如说弗莱的文本里可以看到意态高华，而格林伯格的写作则是一种密不透风的紧

8.

格林伯格肖像

Greenberg's Portrait

9.

格林伯格:《艺术与文化》,沈语冰译,广西师范大学出版社,2009年6月版;2015年修订版

Art and Culture, written by Clement Greenberg and translated by Shen Yubing, Guangxi Normal University Press, June 2009 edition; 2015 revised edition

张感。另外他不像弗莱那样具体地分析作品，他只做一些白热化的断言，譬如"某某是现在仍在世的最伟大的美国画家"，断言背后又不是条理分明的逻辑。他对于学院写作的清规戒律一概弃之，某种意义上他的写作就是他的艺术作品。他吸引了当时美国最有才华的一批批评家，包括两位赫赫有名的女批评家，一位是苏珊·桑塔格，还有一位是罗莎琳·克劳斯。她们每天都等着杂志上刊登格林伯格的文章，如果那天有一杯咖啡，有一篇格林伯格的文章，就觉得那一天没有白活。

格林伯格早年学习文学。他认为过去批评家里面只有两位的文章值得读，一个是大诗人、大批评家 T. S. 艾略特，另外一位是罗杰·弗莱。他是自视很高的一个人，赫伯特·里德、克莱夫·贝尔那帮人根本就不在他眼里。他的文章也很有特点，也不难读——他抛开了学院派写作的一切清规戒律，文风是比较清新明快的。当然前提是要能够熟悉他的那一套叙事，那套语法，熟悉了以后其实是很好读的。很多人认为格林伯格的文章很难读，根本就没法看懂，其实不是这样的。

列奥·施坦伯格：毕加索的窥寐者

与格林伯格齐名的另一位批评家叫列奥·施坦伯格图示10，P20，是一位俄罗斯出生的美国批评家和艺术史家。一位有名的美国记者和评论家汤姆·沃尔夫，在1975年写的一本书叫《画出来的箴言》，把施坦伯格、格林伯格和罗森伯格并称为是 "the kings of 'Cultureburg'"（文化三伯格）。施坦伯格、格林伯格和罗森伯格都是纽约的大批评家。其实施坦伯格和格林伯格还是有些不太一样，因为格林伯格是文学批评家出身，以直接在现场写批评为他的职业；而施坦伯格的主要学术贡献是对于文艺复兴的研究，特别是研究米开朗琪罗和莱昂纳多·达·芬奇方面的权威。施坦伯格对于现代艺术也有很多极其了不起的洞察。了不

10.

施坦伯格肖像　　　　　　　　Leo Steinberg's Portrait

11.

毕加索1904年所作的水彩画　　*Sleeping Woman*, Pablo Picasso,
《睡梦中的女人》　　　　　　watercolor, 1904

起到什么程度呢？我直接引用了别人对他写现代艺术的这本书
——《另类准则》的评价。阿瑟·丹托说："这本书是一个事件，
是我们这个时代精神当中的一种力量。"还有一位很著名的学者
说道："列奥·施坦伯格的《另类准则》是本年度最佳艺术类书
籍，如果说还不是整整十年，或一个世纪的最佳艺术类书籍的
话。"这个评价是极高的，且是有理有据的。他说："这本书的意
义并不在于洞察力的质量——尽管质量非常之高，洞见也极其重
要——而在于风格的丰富、精确与优雅……"这跟我前面讲的有
共同的地方，就是丰富、精确和优雅，"……与列奥·施坦伯格
的心灵相遇，是当代艺术批评所能提供的最富有启示意义的经
验之一。"罗伯特·马瑟韦尔，一位著名的画家，抽象表现主义
的一位大师，对这本书有一个评论："这本书确证了我长期拥有
的一个信念，即施坦伯格不仅是艺术批评家中最明晰和独立的
头脑之一，也是最深刻的头脑之一。即便人们不同意他的观点，
也不得不绝对尊重他。"一个大画家对于批评家的一本书有这么
高的评价，这本身就是一件了不起的事。我看中国没有哪个大
画家对批评家有这么高的评价，很难想象。过去唐宋的时候有，
明代的时候还有点影子，但是到后来就没有了。

我们可以来念一段施坦伯格的批评写作，我认为这是一种高级
的"ekphrasis"。希腊人用语言来描述一个具体的视觉形象的修
辞法叫"ekphrasis"，我们中文有音译过来的翻译称作"艺格敷
词"。我认为它是一种"ekphrasis"，就是面对一个画面，要用
语言把它说得完美无缺，写的语言本身就是一种艺术。比如面
对毕加索1904年的一张水彩图表11, P20，我们都觉得好看，但是写
作的时候除了"好看"说不出别的，我们的语言太苍白了。施坦
伯格是怎么说的呢？就是这么一张很小的水彩画，他说：

> 毕加索一幅蓝色时期的水彩画，画下了23岁的艺术家本人。他没有
> 画艺术家们在通常的自画像当中所画的，他没有探索自己的镜像，
> 也没有带着鄙夷的神情望着观众，更没有眼睁睁地盯着模特儿。他

12.

沈语冰拍摄于毕加索博物馆常设
展现场

Photos of the permanent exhibition of the
Picasso Museum taken by Shen Yubing

> 似乎既不在工作，也不在休息，而是深深地陷入了一种无为之中：看一个熟睡的姑娘。

这是第一段。第二段又说道：

> 姑娘躺在弥漫的光里，一条抬起的手臂枕着她的脑袋。她近在咫尺，却似乎要悄悄溜走，她背后那糊了墙纸的角落也融化在午睡的暖流里。正是画家的形象传达了对这一情景令人忧郁的关注。微暗的蓝色墨水弄平了他的杯子和头发。他那冰冷的阴影与她的明亮恰成对比；他坐着的样子与她平躺着的姿势形成呼应；他那硬朗的身躯又与她敏感的肌肤构成强烈的对照。他们之间的对比是全方位的。正如她的光辉暗示着身体的极大欢悦，他不知所措的意识则成了一种被放逐的状态。

一个画面，两段"ekphrasis"，我认为比希腊人更厉害，他达到了曹子建写《洛神赋》的水平。

施坦伯格的影响非常大。今年暑假我去毕加索博物馆转了一圈，它有一个关于毕加索和考尔德互动的新展览，但是它的最上面两层仍然是毕加索的常设展。这跟策展也有关，其中一层的主题是毕加索的白天，描绘了地中海阳光下的那些人，最上面一层是毕加索的夜晚，而夜晚的主题用的就是列奥·施坦伯格的"sleepwatcher"这个词，就是"窥寐者"。过去的英文辞典里查不到这个词，这是施坦伯格杜撰出来的词，意思是"看人家睡觉的人"。我在翻译的时候，也杜撰了一个中文词，叫"窥寐者"，就是"偷窥人家睡觉的人"。我突然发现在这层的展览说明里引用了这个词，而且策展人提到了列奥·施坦伯格。这说明重要的批评家的思想资源已经运用到现在的策展。那个展览讲的是，毕加索的时间跟别人是黑白颠倒的，别人睡觉的时候他在工作，别人工作的时候他睡觉。他画了大量的在睡觉、做梦、躺着或者专注于自己的事情、沉浸在自己心灵里面的这样一些人物。

13.

迈耶·夏皮罗肖像　　　　　　　　　　Meyer Schapiro's Portrait

还有一幅是一个人躺着，旁边有一个人坐着看着她，就是刚才我们提到的《窥寐者》。策展人在这里用了"窥寐者"这个词，这个词是谁第一个发明的？就是艺术史家列奥·施坦伯格。我拍了几张在四楼展出的毕加索作品，有在夜晚读书的，有躺着的人，还有弥诺陶和美女的作品。这张图是萨蹄尔掀开了宁芙的帐帷，在毕加索的画面里萨蹄尔好像不是一个恶魔或者猛兽，而是变得温柔。弥诺陶也有过这样的行为，当看到美女的时候他不再是野兽，而是变得很温柔了。这一组现在在毕加索博物馆的常设展的第四层展出，这一层的关键就是"窥寐者"，都是跟夜晚、睡眠有关的。刚开始给大家看的那幅，毕加索自己在看一个熟睡的姑娘。这个母题出现在毕加索的笔下，而对于这个母题最好的阐释和批评，我认为到现在没有一个人能超过列奥·施坦伯格。所以我觉得艺术史是这样的，艺术史当然主要是由艺术家创作的作品构成，但是如果没有批评家对于这些作品很好的阐释，深入的挖掘，或者说没有很好的"ekphrasis"，它的传播一定会受到影响。现在当然有各种图片、录像可以帮助传播，但是除非哪一天大家都不用文字了，人类倒退到洞穴时代，那么，它就需要文字，需要批评家。^{图示12，P22}

迈耶·夏皮罗：用现代艺术的眼光重新审视古代艺术

接下来就是迈耶·夏皮罗^{图示13，P24}。他的生卒年代贯穿了20世纪，他是一位立陶宛出生的美国艺术史家。他出名是因为他锻造了新的艺术史的研究方法，这种方法就是把跨学科的研究带到了对于艺术品的审视中。他的研究领域比较广泛，包括了古代晚期、基督教早期的艺术、中世纪艺术和罗马式艺术，还有现代艺术，跨度很大。大多数研究早期基督教艺术或中世纪艺术的古典艺术学者，他们一般看不起现代艺术，认为研究现代艺术不是学问，研究古典艺术才是学问。夏皮罗是一位古典学者，但是他对于现代艺术的研究作出了巨大贡献。

14.

迈克尔·弗雷德肖像　　　　　　　　　Michael Fried's Portrait

15.

《艺术与物性》,《专注性与剧场性》　　*Art and Objecthood: Essage and Review, Absorption and Theatricality: Painting and Beholder in the Age of Diderot*

迈耶·夏皮罗有一个最主要的观点：正因为我们了解了现代艺术，古代艺术里面很多过去被忽略的、没有受到重视的面向和特征才被我们注意到了。这个观念是很先进的，不仅夏皮罗有这个观点，而且我们一开始讲到的意大利那位写《西方艺术批评史》的文杜里也有同样的观点，一切艺术史都是批评史。什么意思呢？如果我们不了解当代艺术，不了解当代正在发生的东西，我们无法倒回去看古代，你会发现不了很多东西。事实上正因为我们了解了马蒂斯、毕加索，回过头才发现，原来黑人土著的面具具有极高的艺术价值；原来拜占庭的宗教画不像我们原来想象的那么僵硬，只是为了传道，拜占庭的艺术也拥有很高的审美价值。因为他们的原理跟现代艺术是相通的，绕过的恰巧是文艺复兴以来那段写实的历史。在文艺复兴的艺术观看来，拜占庭艺术太僵硬太死板了。但是有现代艺术的眼光以后，你会发现中世纪的艺术很有意思。这是夏皮罗的一个重要贡献。夏皮罗生前出了四本自选集，其中两本已经出了中文版。一本是《现代艺术》，还有一本是《艺术的理论与哲学》，另外两本正在组织翻译中。在我翻译过的著作里面，夏皮罗的语言跟罗杰·弗莱的语言一样优美。

迈克尔·弗雷德的《专注性与剧场性》：对狄德罗表演理论的承继与发展

最后，我说一下美国当代一位杰出的艺术批评家迈克尔·弗雷德。图片14，P26。迈克尔·弗雷德和我讲的第一个人狄德罗在思想上有直接的承继关系。弗雷德今年80岁，跟中国也有一些渊源：他们夫妇领养了一名生于武汉的中国女孩。迈克尔·弗雷德在普林斯顿学的是文学，在哈佛大学读的是艺术史博士，在这之间他开始写艺术评论。他的评论非常有名，跟他辩论的那些人里有像格林伯格，T·J·克拉克，罗莎琳·克劳斯这样的一些重要的人物。另外他和美国的哲学家斯坦利·卡维尔维持了终生的友情。我问了一下复旦哲学院的老师，斯坦利·卡维尔的著作至今未有一本被翻译成中文，我觉得也是一个遗憾，要不然我们在讲迈克尔·弗雷德的时候就可以找到一些对谈的人。

迈克尔·弗雷德的著作，我们已经翻译成中文的主要是这两本，一本是《艺术与物性》，一本是2019年刚刚出版的《专注性与剧场性》图示15, P26。我先简单的说一下《艺术与物性》。它一开始是一篇评论文章 "Art and Objecthood"，发表于1967年，后来以这篇文章为题出版了他的评论文集。在这篇文章当中，他认为极简主义聚焦于观众的体验，而不是艺术品的形式特质，或者说形式关系——艺术品本身有各种关系。我们在谈现代艺术的时候，会聚焦于现代艺术作品里面形的关系，色的关系，构图关系等等。但是，我们在看极简主义作品的时候，我们注意的焦点已经不再是作品的形色关系这些问题，而是观众参与的身体体验。所以，他锻造了一个词来形容极简主义，称为 "literalism"，就是"字面上的、实在的、就事论事的"。他说这种艺术提供的是一种剧场的经验，而跟"剧场性"相对应的就是他后面一本书里锻造的一个词叫"专注性"（Absorption）——意思就是有吸引力的，在专注的状态里做一件自己的事情。所以他在《艺术与物性》里面批评极简主义是剧场性的，又在他的另外一本书里面引入对立的一个词，叫"专注性"，所以那本书叫《专注性与剧场性：狄德罗时代的绘画与观众》。他在书里主要是引用了狄德罗的批评，他认为一旦艺术家意识到观众的存在，他的专注就会打折，剧场性就会产生。

这是什么意思呢？狄德罗有一个表演理论：演员应该完全沉浸在自己角色里面，不要考虑到下面有观众在看你，一旦考虑到观众，你的表演就显得做作，你会想主动做出某些效果。我们来具体看一下迈克尔·弗雷德的理论，我从他的一篇关于马奈的论文里摘了一段：

我的书《专注性与剧场性》和《库尔贝的写实主义》，已经追踪了从18世纪中叶到19世纪60年代上半叶为止的法国绘画的反剧场性传统。这是一个什么样的传统呢？这一传统的核心是这样的一种要求，最早是狄德罗在18世纪50年代下半叶和60年代从理论上驾驭美术的。绘画或者是一个舞台场面的（狄德罗把它扩展到了舞台艺术中）人物要不去关注观众，要当观众不存在。这在实践中意味着被再现的人物显得完全沉浸在或者正如我常说的那样，专注于他们的行动、情感和心智状态当中。如此专注的人物会被感到，除了他们自己所专注的事物以外，忘怀一切，包括站在画外的观众。假如艺术家在这个事情当中失败，假如画中的一个或者更多的人物，像是仅仅想要引起人们的震惊，或者以一种有意引起观众注意的态度加以表演，那么其结果是可怕的。不仅人物本身看起来显得做作，而且作为一个整体的画作，从这样的一个角度看也会被认为是一种失败。

法语的这个词 "做作"（théâtral)，其实在当时是一个毁灭性的谴责。这是迈克尔·弗雷德在写马奈的一篇论文里，一段对他的过去的思想的很好的总结，语言极其清晰，但是又很深刻。

伟大的艺术批评具备哪些特质？

讲到这里，我再概括一下伟大批评的一些基本特质。

第一个，就是高度的智性。几乎所有了不起的艺术家、批评家都有这样一个特点，他们都有一种思辨上的高度的智性。思想水平达不到一定的高度成不了一个时代的批评家，事实上也成不了一个时代的画家。我在讲马奈的时候讲到过马奈一生，他早年与波德莱尔，中年与左拉（Émile Zola），后来和马拉美（Stéphane Mallarmé）——三位当时法国最有名的诗人和作家关系密切，后来还与一大帮印象派的画家、批评家朋友来往。马奈不像波德莱尔或者马拉美那样读那么多书，但是他交往的人，是那个时代法国读书最多、头脑最聪明的人，可以这样说，波德莱尔和马拉美帮助马奈达到了思想上的高度。有人提出过一个困扰了中国几十年的问题：艺术家要不要读书？艺术家不需要读书的观点曾经在中国很流行，至少在二、三十年前是这样。后来有所改变，因为现在的艺术家很多都是有 MFA、PhD 学位的，大家现在意识到当代艺术家都是读书的。不读书根本无法成为一位当代艺术家。

第二，就是比较扎实的史学功底，这里面唯一例外的就是格林伯格。格林伯格精通文学史胜过了艺术史。其实他对艺术史不是很了解，但是他对文学史是很精通的，因此也不能说他完全是个例外，他精通文学史，有史学功底。也就是说，你的写作要有历史的厚度和深度。

第三，是一种极其清晰的语言表达，一种辨析的能力。这几乎是所有批评家的特点。中国古人要求好文章要有义理、考据和辞章，义理就是道理的辨析，考据就是要有历史证据，辞章就是文章语言要优美绵密，"言之无文，行而不远"。所以，我现在对于伟大的批评的基本特点的概括，还是中国古人的义理、考据和辞章。但是我赋予它们以新的内涵，那就是从罗杰·弗莱到迈克尔·弗雷德这些批评家的文本所体现的内涵。

我再提一下文杜里说过的一句很有名的话，"艺术批评是我们将艺术品理解为艺术的唯一方式"。这句话是什么意思呢？因为你也可以将艺术品理解为历史材料——现在有很多搞美术考古的人，就是没有将艺术品理解为艺术、不考虑美的问题，只要是能够证明某一段历史的材料就可以了。现在还有一些做视觉文化研究的人，他们当中流行所谓"图像证史"，用图像来证明历史，同样也只是把图像当成了一种材料、手段，而不是图像本身。他们对于图像的好坏、质量，对于图像的形式和风格，对于"ekphrasis"一点也不感兴趣。

如果感兴趣的话，有几本参考书目可以供大家进一步了解这个话题。一本是文杜里的《西方艺术批评史》，另一本是我的《20世纪艺术批评》，写得比较早，最近一次重印是2018年。我还有一本书是2017年商务印书馆出版的《图像与意义：英美现代艺术史论》，从罗杰·弗莱讲到格林伯格、施坦伯格、夏皮罗、T. J. 克拉克、乔纳森·克拉里。最后两个人主要是做纯史学的，所以我今天没有介绍。我认为这些人构成了三代学者，罗杰·弗莱是第一代，施坦伯格、格林伯格和夏皮罗是第二代，T. J. 克拉克和乔纳森·克拉里是第三代，涉及六种治艺术史的方法。此外，我和张晓剑编了《20世纪西方艺术批评文选》，第一版已经脱销了，预计2020年下半年会进行再版。这是从波德莱尔——他属于19世纪，但是我们把他作为20世纪的先驱者——一直到20世纪90年代的一些著名批评家的文本，大概七、八十万字。

艺术批评写作的危机

最后来讲一下危机。艺术批评写作的危机在一开始的时候我已经提到了，但是没有作为重点来谈。危机主要是说面临着一些问题，比如说在我研究的领域里，迈克尔·弗雷德所面临的个人危机。他从当代艺术现象里提炼出了一个重要概念，叫"剧场性"，这是个被公认为当代艺术的基本概念。他很了不起的一点是他能够从极简主义里提炼出这个概念，但是他自己的立场站在了对立面，批评了剧场性。但是后来他发现大多数当代艺术基本都是剧场性的，所以他退出了批评界，1970年代以后开始做法国19世纪的绘画研究，没法再介入当代艺术了。因为当代艺术的发展出乎他的意料，或者说用他的话来讲就是"雪崩式的剧场性"，像雪崩一样，个人无法控制，完全出乎他的意料。这既说明了好的批评所具备的敏锐和提炼概念的能力——从现象里提炼概念是一种大学问家和大批评家的能力；但是也说明了这是一个危机，就是说自从他提出剧场性这个概念以后，大部分艺术在他看来都是剧场性的，都要求观众的身体参与，而他所坚守的现代主义立场就变得不合时宜了。

我曾经做过一个纲要性的讲座："观看之道：从静观、剧场到沉浸"。讲的是"静观"，即古典美学里的一个基本概念，或者叫"沉思"（contemplation），到观众参与式的剧场——这是当代艺术早期观众参与的情况，当下的艺术更加注重沉浸式的体验。这里面有一个问题我没提出来，就是现在的批评显然不是针对一个画面，不再是针对一个画面意义上的"ekphrasis"。而是你到了一个情景当中，你的那种沉浸感如何变成新的"ekphrasis"，或者还需不需要"ekphrasis"。现在最有名的几个批评家——纽约和伦敦的几个批评家——看一个展览，然后发一个视频网上一放，他的 YouTube 或者 Twitter 的粉丝几千万，比所有的评论

16.

沈语冰在"青策计划2019"展览
现场参观，2020年。© 上海当
代艺术博物馆

Shen Yubing at the ECP 2019 exhibition,
2020. ©Power Station of Art

家写的文章关注度都要高。过去人们还在等着格林伯格的文章刊登，现在没有人再等批评家的文章，他们会等"网红"式的批评家，跑到一个展览，发一个视频在网上一挂，就得到几千万的粉丝。这就形成一个危机了。当然还有很多其他的问题，别的学者也提到过，比如现在的运作，策展人已经代替了批评家，批评家还能够做什么事情。现在的策展人都有高度的智慧和运作能力，他背后可能有商业机构在运作，这样的话资本也更多地介入到了当代艺术。似乎有发言权的是有钱的人，而不是特别敏锐、特别睿智的批评家们。

所以，这就是我讲的危机。危机有几个方面的原因，我们需要讨论的，或者要引起注意的是我们面临这些危机的时候，我们是否有克服这些危机的可能和方法。比如说有一种犬儒主义，认为现状已然是这样，都是资本的运作，我们没有办法了。打个比方，电影评论基本上是由资本控制的，因为电影是文化工业，所以很少看到有伟大的电影评论家（也许曾经有过，比如意大利新现实主义和法国新浪潮时期），但总的来说，它属于工业，批评家很少有发言权。但是艺术批评也面临着一个危机，我不知道当代艺术是否正在变成类似电影的文化工业。

我想我就讲到这里，谢谢大家！

This lecture intends to outline the great tradition of Anglo-American art criticism, from Roger Fry to Clement Greenberg, Leo Steinberg, and Meyer Schapiro. This tradition is usually regarded as preceded only by the French tradition from Diderot of mid 18th Century to Baudelaire of mid 19th Century. The lecture involves the classic pieces of writing from this history of Anglo-American art criticism, to analyze what makes amazing writings of criticism, what kind of crises they face in the conditions of contemporary art, and finally the possibilities and ways for art criticism to break through such conditions.

Shen Yubing:
The Great Tradition
of Art Criticism
and its Crisis

Long History and Tradition of Art Criticism

Strictly speaking, I don't think curating and criticism can be fully separated, because in recent years curating has evolved into a form of art criticism, and it requires the critic's vision when selecting artists and showing the horizon of art criticism during the curation.

Art criticism can also provide nutrients for curation, because curation is a relatively new thing compared to the long history and tradition of art criticism. When you read *History of Art Criticism* by Lionello Venturi, you will see that the book starts from ancient Greece and Rome. If we are going to write the history of art criticism in China, we can also go back to the Pre-Qin and Han Dynasties, when there were already sparkles of thoughts and examples of criticism. By the Wei, Jin, and Southern and Northern Dynasties, criticism of literature, poetry, painting, and calligraphy had noticeably reached a high level of self-knowledge. As soon as there were art activities, or at least when art activities entered a relatively public domain, there may be art criticism. Therefore, art criticism has a long history and a great tradition.

Today I'm going to focus on the art criticism tradition established by Britain and the United States over the 100 years in the 20th century, without going to art criticism in ancient China, which, of course, is another long and remarkable tradition. Modern art criticism has two focal points, France from the 18th to the 19th century, and Britain and the United States from the second half of the 19th century to the second half of the 20th century. Before talking about Britain and America, I would like to touch on French art criticism in the 18th and 19th centuries.

I will talk about Roger Fry, Clement Greenberg, Leo Steinberg, Meyer Schapiro, Michael Fried, but without going into details. People who haven't read their books before, may be confused about what I'm going to say. I'll try to select some of the most representative excerpts and share them with you to give you a preliminary idea about what a good critical writing should be like.

In the end, I will talk about a huge crisis for the criticism tradition in the second half of the 20th century to the present day, that criticism no longer seems as important as it was in the 18th, 19th and 20th centuries, and is increasingly replaced by curation. At the same time, criticism also faces many practical problems. During the transition from classical art to modern art, artists were more artisans than intellectuals. There was an unwritten rule that artists did not need to read much. It would be incredible if a painter, such as Paul Cézanne or Pablo Picasso, could speak eloquently or become a best-selling author, because it is a departure from the traditional definition and expectation of painters and artists who should be "silent and hands-on".

However, after the 1960s and 1970s, more and more artists have enrolled in colleges and universities, and some even have a Master's or Doctorate degree of Arts. They have read extensively. In terms of thought and intellect, they no longer need critics to help them have a voice. Artists have the sensitivity and intellectuality as high as critics. As a result, here comes a question: Do we still need criticism? This is a frequently asked question. At the end of my speech, I will leave this question to you for discussion.

Pre-history of Modern Art Criticism: From Diderot and Baudelaire

First, let's briefly revisit French art criticism from the mid-18th century to the mid-19th century, when French art was the center of European art. After the Renaissance, Italy was basically the art center because of Florence, Rome, and Venice. After the 17th century, Italy began to wane, and the art center shifted to Amsterdam, Netherlands. In the 18th and 19th centuries, art flourished mainly in Britain and France. As art prospered, many great philosophers and poets began to engage in the study of art and art history. Since then, art criticism has become a formal art activity, and critical writing has also become a specialized category of writing. Along the way, there are two seminal figures, Denis Diderot in the mid-18th century and Charles Pierre

Baudelaire in the mid-19th century. ^{Fig. 1 & Fig. 2, P6}

When we talk about any history of criticism, we will definitely bring Diderot and Baudelaire up as the key figures. I will talk about Michael Fried, a guru in art history and art criticism still active today, and his main theoretical origin can be directly traced back to Diderot. As a historian and critic, Michael Fried proposed the concept of "theatricality", which has a huge impact on the entire ecology of contemporary art. I will introduce him as one of the key figures in the British and American tradition of art criticism at the end of this lecture.

We all know that Diderot is an encyclopedic scholar and major champion in the French Enlightenment. The *Encyclopédie* edited by Diderot and Jean-Baptiste le Rond d'Alembert caused a huge sensation at the time, because it was a deadly blow to the conservative forces in the religion and feudal empires in France and even Europe. The Enlightenment began to transfer secular authority like the Holy See and the King to reason, and who was the representatives of the reason? It was those intellectuals who participated in public discussions. It was a turning point achieved by the Enlightenment, and Diderot played a very critical role during the process. D'Alembert gave up his share of the editorship after a few volumes, while Diderot stayed, and the *Encyclopédie* attracted almost all the major intellectuals in France and even Europe to contribute. Their reorganization of knowledge is a farewell to the previous knowledge system established by theocracy and kingship. It is undeniably a revolution of the mind. Therefore, Diderot was important for his remarkable role in the

Enlightenment. More importantly, he had a huge impact on art criticism: he was the first to write criticism on paintings exhibited in the French salon every year and to publish criticism on newspapers and periodicals. As a bridge and an intermediary, he used his art criticism to establish connections between official exhibitions and the citizenry as well as middle-class households who subscribed to newspapers and magazines. He wrote very high-quality art criticism, so did Diderot, Rousseau and Montesquieu. Their writings are very inspirational and thrilling, unlike the later academic writing which is methodical, and heavy on evidence, logic and reasoning. At that time, most of the writers were novelists and dramatists, who transferred the language and passion of novels, dramas, and poetry to art criticism. This is also one of the reasons why their works are profoundly influential. I will come to the requirement of language and writing skills in art criticism writing in a moment, and will return to Diderot's key idea of criticism when I talk about Michael Fried later.

By the middle of the 19th century, France became dominant in the history of thought and art in Europe. Baudelaire was the most outstanding French poet in the mid-19th century, and gained huge influence not only because of his poetry, but also largely because of his art criticism. Baudelaire wrote a very famous essay, *The Painter of Modern Life*, in which he used the word "modernity" for the first time in history. In the 21st century, we are still discussing modernity, which can be traced back to this poet and critic in the mid-19th century. He was also the first poet to translate Edgar Allan Poe's poetry into French. Almost all modern poets are translators, at least with no exceptions among modern poets in Europe. It may be the same in China, e.g. Mu Dan, that almost all great poets living in and after the Republic of China translated, because they needed to polish their language and understand differences and similarities between different languages through translation to develop language sensitivity. It is a very interesting phenomenon.

Baudelaire's best-known poetry collection is *The Flowers of Evil,* in which he expresses the constantly changing nature of beauty in a rapidly industrialized city, Paris. He subverted the classic aesthetics and traditional concept of "beauty is eternal" adhered to by academism, and believed that beauty changes with the times. But he did not simply make a binary opposition between the permanence of beauty held by traditionalists and the relativity of beauty maintained by romantics. Instead, he made a very intelligent reconciliation. He said that part of beauty is constantly changing, and part of it is eternal. My understanding is that although the times are changing and many things change fast, there are still some things that stay the same, e.g. the fundamental human nature is unalterable. Perhaps what has changed is how culture shapes us. Therefore, Baudelaire cleverly said that beauty is eternal in one way, and changes with the times in another way. In particular, he mentioned that extracting eternity from fleeting phenomena is a tremendous skill; and the fleeting phenomena, fluidity, and changes are "modernity" in his view. Because the word "modernity" originally meant fashion, yet fashion changes the fastest, every year and every season. How do you extract eternal, unchangeable things from fashion? The core concept he puts forward is the eternity in modernity—the dialectic of the immutable and the fleeting. It is a key idea, which I think has not only influenced the poet himself, but also artist Édouard Manet and the entire modern art through Manet, that is, Impressionism and then modern art. In a sense, if we must find the original concept of modern art, its origin is Baudelaire. This is the pre-history of the British and American criticism tradition of the 20th century that I wanted to talk about, starting with Diderot and Baudelaire. France had a vibrant art ecology, including art production, exhibition, consumption, and the largest group of art critics. Once the salon opened, the French newspapers were flooded with criticism about a painter in the salon. For example, when Manet's *Olympia* was exhibited, 73 critics about it were published in the newspapers and magazines in Paris and across France. Now it may take a large biennial to generate an equivalent amount of coverage and criticism, and it is hard to imagine to have so much attention and influence because of only a painter or a piece of his work. Therefore, simply from the figure, we can have a rough idea how much the French at that time cared about salon exhibitions and how much they cared about art. Now even France may not have an artist as influential as Manet. At that time, France saved a large space for culture, which shrank more and more over time. This is the general picture of French art criticism from the mid-18th century to the mid-19th century.

Roger Fry: Leading Figure in British and American Modern Art Criticism

I also focus on British and American modern art criticism

after the 20th century in my research. I'll start with Roger
Fry, and give you an outline of art criticism during this
period, including what the tradition of British and American
modern art criticism from my perspective, who the main
leaders are, and finally what the common characteristics
of these criticisms are, and what enlightenment they have
brought us. Roger Fry was born in the late 19th century
and died in 1934 ^{Fig. 3, P10}. He is the most influential critic
in the history of British and American modern art, and
also a well-known expert of Italian classical painting
connoisseurship. Before appointed as the director of the
European Painting Department of the Metropolitan Museum
of Art of New York City (the Met), he was already recognized
as one of the experts of authority in European classical
painting connoisseurship together with Bernard Berenson
from the United States and Morelli from Italy. Interestingly
enough, Fry made higher achievements later, not in classical
art connoisseurship, but in modern art criticism and in
laying the foundation of modernist aesthetics. He was also
a painter. He studied natural sciences in the University
of Cambridge before going to France and Italy to study
painting, and later became an expert in the connoisseurship
of Italian paintings. He painted continuously and also held
exhibitions until he saw Cézanne's original work in 1906,
the year when Cézanne died. He was shocked to find that
someone had painted something he dreamed of. Therefore,
Fry made a very bold and remarkable decision that he gave
up the opportunity to become the future Director of the Met
and a classical scholar, and chose to defend the nascent
modern art which was far from being generally recognized
by scholars and critics in Europe at that time, not to
mention by the general public.

In 1910 and 1912, Roger Fry organized two Post-Impressionist exhibitions in London. The word "Post-Impressionism" was termed by Fry himself and is an important reason for critics to enter history. In his time, critics named the early modern art school whatever they wanted, and many of the words they used were derogatory. For example, "Impressionism" and "Fauvism" were made up by critics to pour scorn on those avant-garde painters. In the end, the painters decided to display their works under the name "Impressionism" starting from the third exhibition out of the eight they organized. "Post-Impressionism" was coined by Roger Fry to include Cézanne and the painters after Cézanne to distinguish it from Impressionism. Roger Fry was also the first scholar who was both a critic and curator in the true sense. He and his assistant Clive Bell went to Europe to select artists and their works in person. Clive Bell later wrote a book *Art*, in which he proposed a concept called "significant form". It was a slogan that was very popular in the circle of aesthetics in the 1980s China. Now many people who work on aesthetic research only know about Clive Bell, but don't know Roger Fry. In fact, Clive Bell was Roger Fry's assistant, and Roger Fry was first entrusted to write the book by a publishing house. However, Roger Fry was not keen to write such a purely theoretical book, so he left the assignment to Clive Bell, who was from the generation of his students. Young and ambitious, Clive Bell overthrew all the theories of European classical aesthetics in his book. Classical aesthetics maintains that art is determined by the subject and theme, but Bell believed that it is not the subject or theme but the form that determines art, namely, art is a "significant form". His point of view has such a tremendous impact that he is considered a representative of formalist aesthetics. However, in fact behind him, there was Bloomsbury Group, a London intellectual collective joined by Roger Fry and led by Virginia Woolf. Bloomsbury was an elite coterie of novelists, economists, poets, painters, critics, aestheticians, and philosophers, and Fry and Woolf were two leading members. Roger Fry made very high achievements. A historian Kenneth Clark, who succeeded Fry as Slade Professor of Fine Art at Cambridge and Oxford, has a famous comment about Fry, that he "is incomparably the greatest influence on taste since John Ruskin. In so far as taste can be changed by one man, it was changed by Roger Fry." It is the highest compliment and I think it is pertinent, because Fry changed the general aesthetic interest or the so-called taste of the British public since Ruskin, allowing Britain to catch up with France and bringing an end to the state of being a culturally isolated island.

Some of Roger Fry's major works have been translated into Chinese, which are the literature we can't avoid when teaching the history of art history and criticism in the 20th century. You can have a look at them. For example, *Cézanne: A Study of His Development* [Fig. 4, P10], written in his later years. This book is hailed by Virginia Woolf as Fry's greatest work. We have collected all the articles he wrote to defend Post-Impressionism and translated them into Chinese. I have summarized several main characteristics of Fry's writing, which may not be precise. First, high intelligence and keen sensitivity. He was a historian and studied Italian classical art in his early years. He was also a painter and studied in natural sciences. He was a member of a secret Society of King's College, Cambridge. Each year, the Society would anonymously select a freshman of King's College to join the group. Members met every Saturday and one of them would talk about his idea about a book, and took fierce criticism from all the graduate or undergraduate elites selected by King's College. The speaker would have to defend himself against the criticism. Members were trained in this way to achieve certain level of intelligence. Years later, people finally found out who was in this group, and Roger Fry was one of them. Second, precise, explicit and elegant language with the demeanor of an English gentleman. I will read you a few paragraphs of his criticism in a moment, and you will see that that is how a real critic should debate—in his own pace and with a restrained or courteous tone, he managed to subtly alter the reader's view. It is a great way to write. Finally, strong empathic capability. For example, when I translated his writing about Cézanne, I often wondered: was he writing about Cézanne or himself? He was so empathic with Cézanne's works and that you sometimes don't know if he was writing Cézanne or himself. Without such empathy, I don't think anyone can write first-rate criticism.

If you have read some of Fry's articles, you will understand how elegant his writing is and how brilliant his argument is. For example, when he opposes the imitation theory of Impressionism, he writes:

> Post-Impressionism has begun to abandon the
> faithful reproduction, or let's say, faithful imitation
> of Impressionism, so people will naturally ask the
> questions, why should artists recklessly abandon all the
> science about painting that mankind have had since the
> Renaissance? Why do Post-Impressionists seek to return

to primitive art and start to absorb non-Western 'primitive art', or 'barbaric art' as was ridiculed by people? The answer is that it is neither willfulness nor recklessness, but inevitability, if art is to be freed from the growing hopeless swell of its own scientific methods, and to regain the power of expressing thoughts and emotions, rather than resorting to the curiosity and amazement at the artist's dangerous skills.

This answer is very clever, because he reasons in a language acceptable to readers. He continues:

Modern art has come to Impressionism, where it can depict anything visible with unprecedented convenience and precision, and it is also there, while giving precise visual value to any part of the painting and describing any human import of the depicted things, it is trapped in a powerless situation.

He believes that Impressionism is almost as precise as the camera in terms of reproduction, but it is impotant when delivering the human import of the depicted things. So, he says:

It can't materially change the visual value of an object, because the whole is here, and second only to it. But it is necessary to reassess the phenomenon to provide the depiction of nature with the ability to respond to human passion and human needs, not according to pure vision, but the preset requirements of human reason.

In addition to pure vision, it must also comply with human reason, that is, to be connected with human intellectuality, so it is considered an important contribution of Cézanne to not paint what the eyes see, i.e. vision, but readjust it. This is why Fry's another criticism publication is called *Vision and Design*, that is, to give vision a structural texture. Vision is perceptual, and design is intellectual. In this way, Roger Fry clearly explained the issue in a few simple words.

Another example is how Fry responded to Mr. Holliday. Holliday criticized Cézanne's *The Bather*^{Fig. 5, P14} for having too many lines, and believed that the lines should be hidden according to the tradition of classical painting. Fry so refuted Holliday's criticism:

> *From this perspective, he was completely right about Cézanne's "The Bather", but unfortunately, Mr. Holliday pushed it too far. Almost everything he said applies to Raphael's Sketch of "The Virgin and Child"* ^{Fig. 6, P14}*. If Mr. Holliday wants to maintain the consistency of his position, he must say that for those who have seen a woman's head, who has seen a few outlines on her oval face? Who has seen the lines of the skull shown under her hair? Who has seen so many parallel dark hachures on her cheeks? He will certainly make this and that criticism. He forgets that art takes the reproduction of nature as a means of expression, but reproduction itself is not the purpose, so it cannot be a criterion for criticism.*

Fry skillfully and effectively refuted the opposite opinion with a few sentences that if you say that Cézanne is wrong for using too many lines in his character, please look at Raphael's sketch, where there are a lot of parallel hachures in the Virgin May's face. Should there be so many dark lines in a woman's face? Therefore, all paintings are merely something created based on media and conventions. I think it is very impressive of Roger Fry to prove Mr. Holliday wrong with a few words and it may come from the training the gentleman received at King's College, Cambridge.

The above belongs to Roger Fry's theoretical work in defense of the Post-Impressionism. I quoted his comment on Cézanne in four parts, which are actually in the same paragraph in his book. He talks about Cézanne's early work *The Banquet* Fig. 7, P16, which is also called *The Orgy*, which is a group of drunken, naked men and women. Cézanne saw many Baroque paintings in museums, but he had no idea how those paintings were created. He was taught by no one but himself, so everything from his composition to character modeling is a mess. However, according to Fry, Cézanne's use of color is excellent:

The paint is quite heavy due to many layers of brushstrokes. The beholder can see the traces of Cézanne's determined handwriting, as well as the painful efforts he made for his dream to come true. Anyway, his brushstrokes are always clear and refined, and the colors always bright and pure. However, people can get a glimpse of how the heroism of this extraordinary character can make the most absurd statement of phenomena with such uncompromising frankness and determined confidence. People can also see his unfailing talent: his impeccable sense of color. Even when he works desperately for some natural reproduction and realistic verisimilitude, every one of his strokes is never missed, either enhancing the harmony of the work or enriching the creative ensemble of colors. It is in his color that we can find his most fundamental quality, as well as the primary source of inspiration for his modeling creativity. Color sense is an essential quality of Cézanne, and was kept at an absolutely great level in any case. This work is perhaps the earliest manifesto, promising one of Cézanne's greatest contributions to art, that is, he believes that color is not something attached to or imposed on form, but is an idea about a direct component of form.

Therefore, Fry believes that although Cézanne's early works failed at composition and character modeling, his color sense is first-rate. I think we always feel excited when looking at Cézanne's works, but we cannot tell why. Then we have Roger Fry who has explained it all in words.

Greenberg: Master of Formalist Aesthetics

It is Clement Greenberg [Fig. 8, P18] who brought Roger Fry's formalist aesthetics to the extreme. After the rise of Postmodernism, all accusations were fired at him. Greenberg is a seminal figure closely linked with the history of American modern art in the 20th century. He built up formalist aesthetics, and is of course, best known for his views on abstract expressionism and his personal relationship with Jackson Pollock. Greenberg's only self-selected publication before his death is *Art and Culture* [Fig. 9, P18].

Although Greenberg and Fry share something in common, e.g. their languages are both precise, concise and explicit, he and Fry are different in some ways. For example, Greenberg's words create a sense of suffocating tenseness, while Fry's writing is elegant and tasteful. In addition, Greenberg does not analyze works as specifically as Fry, but only makes heated assertions with no clear logic, such as "someone is the greatest living American painter". He completely abandoned the rules of academic writing. In a sense, his writing is his work of art. He attracted the most talented critics in the United States at that time, including two famous female critics, Susan Sontag and Rosalind Krauss. They waited for Greenberg's article to come out in the magazine every day. For them, life was not wasted if there was a cup of coffee and an article by Greenberg that day.

Greenberg studied literature in his early years. He believed that only two critics' articles from the past were worth reading, one was the great poet and critic T.S. Eliot, and the other was Roger Fry. Greenberg was a person with high self-esteem, and completely ignored people like Herbert Read and Clive Bell. His essays are also characteristic and readable because he abandoned all rules for academic writing and therefore, his style is fresh and bright, provided of course, that you are already familiar with his narrative and grammar. Many people think that Greenberg's articles are difficult to read and simply incomprehensible, which is not true.

Leo Steinberg: Picasso's Sleepwatcher

Another critic on par with Clement Greenberg is Leo Steinberg [Fig. 10, P20], a Russian-born American critic and art historian. A well-known American journalist and critic, Tom Wolfe, wrote in his book *The Painted Word* in 1975, calling Leo Steinberg, together with Clement Greenberg and Harold Rosenberg the "Kings of 'Cultureburg'". They three were all great critics in New York. Nevertheless, Steinberg is a bit different from Greenberg, because Greenberg was a literary critic, and professionally wrote onsite criticism, while Steinberg made main academic contribution to the Renaissance research, especially on artists such as Michelangelo and Leonardo da Vinci, and had an extraordinary insight into modern art. How extraordinary? I'll quote some reviews on Steinberg's book *Other Criteria*. According to Arthur Coleman Danto, "this book is an event and a power in the spirit of our time." Another famous scholar applauded: "Leo Sternberg's *Other Criteria* is the best art book of the year, if not the decade or the century", a review that is extremely high and well-founded, and he continued, "The point about this book is not the quality of insight—its insight is quality and significant—but the richness of style, precision and elegance..." This echoes with what I said before, i.e. rich, precise and elegant. "... meeting with Leo Steinberg, soul to soul, is one of the most inspiring experience that modern art criticism can ever provide." Robert Matherwell, a famous painter and master of abstract expressionism, made a comment: "It confirms my long-held belief that Steinberg is not only one of the most clear-minded and the most independent among all the art critics, but also one of the most profound. Even if people do not agree with him, they must absolutely respect him." It is remarkable enough for a great painter like him to give such a high evaluation of a book written by a critic. I don't think there is any famous painter in China who thinks this highly of critics. It is simply difficult to imagine. There were some in the Tang and Song Dynasties, and much fewer in the Ming Dynasty, while later there is none.

Let's read a few sentences from Steinberg's criticism writing, which I think is advanced "ekphrasis". The Greeks called the language description of a specific visual image "ekphrasis", which is " 艺格敷词 " when transliterated into Chinese. I think it is "ekphrasis", because if you can perfectly depict the image in front of you in language, then the writing language is art in its own right. For example, looking at the watercolor painted by Picasso in 1904 [Fig. 11, P20], we know it is beautiful, but our language is too pale that all we can write is "beautiful". What does Steinberg say about this small-size watercolor painting? He says:

"This watercolor from Picasso's Blue Period records the 23-year-old artist himself. He did not paint what artists usually painted in self-portraits. He did not explore his mirror image, nor did he look contemptuously at the audience or straightly at the model. He seemed to be neither at work nor resting, but fell deep into a state of inaction: looking at a sleeping girl."

This above is the first paragraph, and he continues in the second paragraph:

The girl lies in diffused light, her head pillowed on her raised arm. She seems so close, yet so likely to sneak away. The wallpapered corner behind her also melts in the warm nap atmosphere. It is the painter's image that conveys melancholic attention to this scene. The dull blue ink smoothens his cup and hair, and his cold shadow highlights her brightness; his sitting posture echoes her flat body lying down; his tough body sharply contrasts with her sensitive skin. The contrast between them is comprehensive. Just as her radiance hints at her great physical joy, his perplexity puts him in a state of exile.

One image, two paragraghs of ekphrasis. I think Steinberg is even more impressive than the Greeks, because his writing is comparable to Cao Zijian's *The Goddess of the Luo*.

Steinberg is very influential. I visited the Picasso Museum this summer. There was a new exhibition about the interaction between Picasso and Alexander Calder, but on the top two floors there were still Picasso's permanent exhibitions, which is also associated with the curation. The exhibition theme on the top second floor is Picasso's daytime series, depicting people under the Mediterranean sun, and that on the top floor features Picasso's night works, under the term invented by Leo Sternberg, "sleepwatcher". This word was not included in the English dictionary before and coined by Sternberg. It means "the one who watches others sleeping". While I was translating, I also coined a Chinese word, "窥寐者", which means "the one who steals a glance at the sleeper". I found that the term was quoted in the exhibition introduction on this floor, and the curator mentioned Leo Steinberg. It shows that this important critic's thought has been applied to modern curation. The exhibition is about Picasso working at night while others slept and sleeping while others worked. He created a large number of characters, sleeping, dreaming, lying down or focusing on their own things, and being lost in their own minds. There is also this one, in which a woman lies down and a man sits next to her, looking at her, which is *Sleepwatcher* we just mentioned. The curator used the term "sleepwatcher" here. Who invented the term first? Art historian Leo Steinberg did. I took a few pictures of Picasso's works on the fourth floor, some depicting characters reading at night, some lying down, and also the one about Minotaur and the beauty. In this picture, Satyrs lifted Nymph's bed drapery. In Picasso's painting, Satyr is not like a demon or beast, but looks gentle. Minotaur is also given such behavior in another painting by Picasso that when Minotaur sees the beauty, he is no longer a beast, but becomes very gentle. This collection is now on show in the permanent exhibition on the fourth floor of the Picasso Museum. The key work on this floor is "sleepwatcher", and all the works are related to night and sleep. In the painting I showed you earlier, Picasso was watching a sleeping girl. This motif often appears in Picasso's creation, and I don't think anyone else so far can give a better interpretation and criticism of this motif than Leo Steinberg. So, I think art history is like this. Certainly, art history is mainly composed of works created by artists, but if there were no good interpretation, in-depth exploration or good "ekphrasis" of these works by critics, the dissemination of the works would undoubtedly be limited. We can turn to pictures and videos to circulate now, but works of art need words and critics until one day humans should stop using words and regress to cavemen Fig. 12, P24 .

Meyer Schapiro: Reexamining Antique Art from the Perspective of Modern Art

Next we are going to talk about Meyer Schapiro Fig. 13, P25 . He lived through the 20th century. He was a Lithuanian-born American art historian. He is well known for the new research method of art history he created, that is to bring interdisciplinary research to the examination of artworks.

He had an extensive research area across a broad spectrum, including late antique, early Christian and medieval art, Romanesque art, as well as modern art. Most classical art scholars who study early Christian art or medieval art generally look down on modern art, thinking that unlike classical art research, modern art research is not an academic subject. Schapiro is a classical scholar, but he has made great contributions to the study of modern art.

Meyer Schapiro holds a major point that it is precisely because of the study of modern art that we start to see many aspects and features of antique art that were previously overlooked and ignored. It is a very advanced idea. Not only Schapiro, but also Lionello Venturi, the Italian author of *History of Art Criticism* whom we mentioned in the beginning, has the same view. Art history is a history of criticism. What does that mean? If we don't understand modern art or what's happening in the modern times, we can't revisit ancient times and learn much. In fact, it is exactly because we understand Matisse and Picasso that we realize that the masks of black natives have extremely high artistic value when we look back; Byzantine religious paintings are not just for preaching and not as rigid as we thought, and Byzantine Art also has a high aesthetic value. Because they shared the same principles of modern art, they all avoided the history of realism since the Renaissance. From the perspective of Renaissance art, Byzantine art is too rigid. However, with the vision of modern art, you will find medieval art very interesting. It is an important contribution of Schapiro. During his lifetime, Schapiro had four publications, two of which have been published in Chinese, one is *Modern Art* and the other is *Theory and*

Philosophy of Art. The other two books are being translated. From the works I have translated, Schapiro's language is as beautiful as Roger Fry's.

Michael Fried's *Absorption and Theatricality*: Succession and Development of Diderot's Performance Theory

Finally, I'm going to talk about Michael Fried [Fig. 14, P26], an outstanding contemporary art critic in America. Michael Fried has a direct inheritance relationship of thought with Diderot, the first critic I talked about today. Fred is 80 years old now and also has some connections with China— he and his wife adopted a Chinese girl born in Wuhan. Michael Fried studied literature at Princeton University and a Ph.D. in Art History at Harvard University, during which he began to write art reviews. His reviews are very famous, and he debated with some important figures such as Clement Greenberg, T.J. Clark, and Rosalind Krauss. In addition, he and American philosopher Stanley Cavell maintained a lifelong friendship. I checked with a teacher of the School of Philosophy, Fudan University that none of Stanley Cavell's works has been translated into Chinese, which is a pity. Otherwise we could include some of his argument when we talk about Michael Fried.

The two works of Michael Fried that have been translated to Chinese are *Art and Objecthood* and *Absorption and Theatricality*, which was recently published in 2019 [Fig. 15, P26]. Let me briefly talk about *Art and Objecthood*, which was originally published in 1967 as a review, and later as his namesake criticism collection. In the review, he believes that minimalism focuses on the audience's experience, rather than the formal characteristics or the formal relationship of the artwork, that is, the relational properties of the artwork. When we talk about modern art, we focus on the relationship between form, color, composition etc. However, when we look at the minimalist works, our focus shifts from the relationship between form and color of the work to the physical experience of the audience. Therefore, he coined the word "literalism" to describe minimalism, which means "literally, practically, matter-of-factly". He said that this kind of art provides a theatrical experience, and he invented another word "absorption", as the opposite of "theatricality" in his next book, denoting the state of being absorbed in doing your own thing. That's why he criticizes minimalism for being theatrical in *Absorption and Theatricality*, and introduces "absorption" in his next book in opposition to "theatricality". It also explains why the book is entitled *Absorption and Theatricality: Painting and Beholder in the Age of Diderot*. He mainly quotes Diderot's criticism in this book, and believes that once the artist realizes the existence of the audience, his concentration will decline and theatricality will emerge.

What does it mean? Diderot has a performance theory that the actor should be completely immersed in his role and pay no attention to his audience. Once he cares about the audience, his performance will be pretentious, because he would like to voluntarily create certain effects. Let's take a closer look at Michael Fried's theory. Here is an excerpt from his essay on Manet:

> *My books, 'Absorption and Theatricality' and 'Courbet's Realism' have traced the anti-theatricality tradition of*

French paintings from the mid-18th century to the first half of the 1860s. What kind of tradition is it? The core of this tradition is the requirement first applied by Diderot to fine art in a theoretical sense in the second half of the 1850s and the 1860s. Characters in a painting or stage scene (which was extended to stage art by Diderot) should pay no attention to and take no notice of the existence of the audience. In practice, it means that the reproduced characters should be completely immersed in, or as I often say, absorbed in their actions and states of emotions and mind. Such attentive characters can be felt. They are so attentive that they forget everything but the things they focus on, including the audience standing in front of the painting. If the artist fails on this, and if one or more characters in a painting seem to try to amaze people, or act in a way to attract attention, the result is terrible. Not only does the person appear to be artificial, but also the painting as a whole will be considered a failure in this aspect.

The French word *théâtral* was actually a devastating condemnation at the time. Quoted from in his essay on Manet, the above is a good summary of Fried's thoughts. His language is extremely explicit yet profound.

What Are the Qualities of Great Art Criticism?

Now I will summarize some basic characteristics of great criticism.

First, high intellectuality. Almost all great artists and critics have such a high level of critical intellectuality. Without profound thought, one cannot become a critic of an era, and in fact, nor can he become a painter of an era. When I talked about Manet, I introduced Manet's whole life. He had a close relationship with Baudelaire, Émile Zola, and Stéphane Mallarmé, three of France's most famous poets and writers at that time, respectively in his early years, middle age, and later years. Later he also interacted with a large group of Impressionist painters and critics. Manet did not read as many books as Baudelaire or Mallarmé, but the people he interacted with were the most read and smartest people in France of that era. Therefore, we can say that Baudelaire and Mallarmé helped Manet reach the profundity of thinking. Someone asked a question that has plagued China for decades: Do artists need to read? The idea that artists do not need to read was once popular in China, at least twenty or thirty years ago. It has changed since many artists now have MFA and PhD degrees, and people are aware that contemporary artists are well-read. One cannot become a contemporary artist if he does not read.

Second, solid historical knowledge. The only exception may be Greenberg, who is better at literary history than art history. In fact, he knows little about art history, but is an expert in literary history, so he is not really an exception with his proficiency in literature history and solid historiographical background. In other words, a critic's writing should have historical profundity and depth.

Third, explicit language expression, i.e. the ability to think and analyze. It is a characteristic possessed by almost all critics. Ancient Chinese thought a good essay must have good argumentation, textural research, and wording. Argumentation means philosophical reasoning, textual research means referring to historical evidence, and wording means elegant critical language. "Words without elegance will not reach far and wide". Therefore, my summary of the basic characteristics of great criticism is consistent with the ancient Chinese criteria of good argumentation, evidence, and expression, but I have given them new connotations, which are embodied in the criticism writings by critics from Roger Fry to Michael Fried.

I would like to give a famous quote of Venturi, "Art criticism is the only way to see art as art." What does it mean? It implies that you can also see art as historical materials. Many art archaeologists do not see art as art or consider beauty. A work of art matters to them only when it is an evidence that can prove a certain history. There are also people who study visual culture. The so-called "use of images to prove history" is popular among them. By doing so, they also view images as merely materials or means, instead of the images themselves. They are not interested in the quality, form or style of images; nor are they interested in "ekphrasis".

If you are interested, here are several books for your further understanding of this topic, one is *History of Art Criticism* by Lionello Venturi and the other is *Art Criticism in the 20th Century* by me, which was written relatively early and recently reprinted in 2018. Another book by me is *Image and Meaning: Historiography of Modern British and American Art History* published by the Commercial Press last year, which talks about critics from Roger Fry to Clement Greenberg, Leo Steinberg, Meyer Schapiro, T. J. Clark, to Jonathan

Crary. The last two critics address pure historiography, so I did not include them today. In my view, these scholars constitute three generations of art critics, with Roger Fry as the first generation, Steinberg, Greenberg, and Schapiro the second, and T. J. Clark and Jonathan Crary the third, involving six methods of studying art history. In addition, Zhang Xiaojian and I co-edited *Selected Works of Western Art Criticism in the 20th Century*. The first edition is out of stock and is expected to be reprinted in the second half of 2020. We collected articles by famous critics from the outset of the 20th century to the 1990s, which is about seventy to eighty thousand words. We also include Baudelaire, who is from the 19th century, but we see him as a pioneer of the 20th century.

Crisis of Art Criticism Writing

Finally, let's talk about the crisis. I have mentioned it in the beginning, but did not focus on it. The crisis refers to the problems, such as the personal crisis facing Michael Fried from the perspective of my research. He refined an important concept from the phenomenon of contemporary art, and termed it as "theatricality", which is recognized as a basic concept of contemporary art. What is remarkable about him is that he refined this concept from minimalism, and then stood against it and criticized theatricality. However, he later discovered that most contemporary art is basically theatrical, so he withdrew from criticism and began to study French paintings in the 19th century after the 1970s, and no longer engaged in contemporary art. He did so, because the development of contemporary art was beyond his expectations, or in his words, embraced "avalanche-like theatricality". Like an avalanche, contemporary art cannot be controlled by any individual, which was completely beyond his expectations. It not only proves that good critical sensitivity and capability of refining concepts, i.e. refining concepts from phenomena, is what a great scholar and critic should be equipped with; but it also shows a crisis. After he proposed the concept of theatricality, most works of art are theatrical in his view, because they require the audience's physical participation, which puts the modernist position he adhered to out of place.

I once gave an outline lecture, "Ways of Seeing: From Contemplation, Theatricality, to Immersion". During my lecture, I talked about "contemplation", a basic concept in classical aesthetics, and audience participation in theatricality, which is about audience participation at the early stage of contemporary art, and immersive experience highlighted by the art now. There is one problem I did not bring up, that is obviously, the current criticism no longer focuses an image or ekphrasis of an image. Instead, at a scene, how does your sense of immersion become new ekphrasis, or do you need ekphrasis at all? Some of the most famous critics nowadays—those in New York and London—post a video online after they visit an exhibition. His YouTube channel or Twitter account has tens of millions of followers, and has higher visibility than any articles written by all critics altogether. In the past, people waited for Greenberg's articles to come out, but now, no one waits for criticism any more. They will wait for popular online critics to go to an exhibition and post a video, which will be viewed by tens of millions of followers. In consequence, it creates a crisis. There are many other problems that other scholars have also mentioned. For example, under the current operation, curators have replaced critics. What else can critics do? Now curators have wisdom and operational capabilities. They may be backed by businesses, which means more capital is involved in contemporary art. It seems that it is the rich who have the say, rather than critics who have sensitivity and wisdom.

So, this is the crisis I am talking about. There are several reasons for the crisis. What we need to discuss or draw attention to is if we have the possibility and method of overcoming the crisis when we face it. There is this cynicism, claiming that it is what it is and nothing can be done in the face of capital operation. For example, movie reviews are largely controlled by capital, because movies are part of the culture industry, and it is rare to see great movie critics in the industry (perhaps there were some during the Italian Neorealism and the French New Wave). In general, movies belong to the industry, and critics rarely have a say. Art criticism also faces a crisis. I don't know if contemporary art is transforming into another culture industry similer to the film industry.

So much for today. Thank you!

青策充电站
联合主办：上海当代艺术博物馆、复旦大学哲学学院

工作团队
上海当代艺术博物馆：张琍莉、马慧婷、徐辰斐、邱鼎、黄彦娜
复旦大学哲学学院：袁新、林晖、沈奇岚、陈佳

实录册编辑团队
编辑：马慧婷、蔺佳
平面设计：邵君瑜
翻译：曾晨
校对：阮汇善

ECP Charging Station Programme
Co-organizers: Power Station of Art,
School of Philosophy, Fudan University

Programme Team
Power Station of Art: Zhang Lili, Ma Huiting, Xu Chenfei,
Qiu Ding, Huang Yanna
School of Philosophy, Fudan University: Yuan Xin, Lin Hui,
Shen Qilan, Chen Jia

Editorial Team
Editor: Ma Huiting, Lin Jia
Graphic Design: Shao Junyu
Translator: Zen Chen
Proofreader: Ruan Huishan

青策充电站
策展与艺术哲学
工作坊

实录

ECP Charging
Station
Workshop Series:
Curating and
Philosophy of Art

Record

独立策展人比利安娜·思瑞克的讲座主要围绕她对策展的认知以及在中国的策展实践展开。本土语境下的展览历史是思瑞克近二十年的策展实践中始终关注的对象。以1979年至2006年间艺术家在上海自发组织的展览历史梳理与研究为起点，再到展览之外不同知识生产形式的探索，思瑞克将通过一系列实践案例分享，阐述其工作方法以及对策展的认知。

比利安娜
思瑞克：
策展及其紧迫性

感谢 PSA 的邀请。我在刚开场的时候先请在座各位青年策展人回答了两个很实际的问题：你在做什么工作？以何为生？ 2000年前后，我在上海开始了策展实践，今时今日整个大环境和工作条件对于刚走上策展道路的年轻人而言已然大不相同，因此我很关注各位是如何在实际工作层面应对现实问题的。今天的演讲将主要围绕我在中国的一系列策展实践展开 —— 本土语境是如何构成了我的策展工作，并形成了我对策展的认知。

基于上海展览史研究的策展实践：重访、激活、生产

自2013年起，我发起了以中国和东南亚地区为关注重心的研讨会平台"从展览的历史到展览制造的未来 —— 中国与东南亚地区"。最近，这个长期的研究项目在召开最后一次研讨会后告一段落，我将研究成果集结成册，出版了一本同名书籍，重新审视了展览作为一种形式和媒介的重要性，并通过邀请写作者、策展人和艺术从业者围绕特定展览建立档案，在不同的社会和文化语境下讨论艺术家自我组织的展览对当地产生的重要影响。关于这个项目的发展，我会在最后再和大家展开分享。更早以前，我编写过一本《上海展览史：1979—2006》^{图示1, P4}，集中收录了1979年至2006年间艺术家在上海组织发起的展览，本书由英

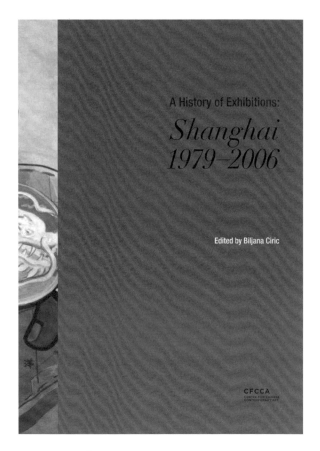

1. 比利安娜·思瑞克:《上海展览史:
1979—2006》,曼彻斯特华人艺
术中心2014年出版。除特殊注明
外,本文内所有图片均由比利安
娜·思瑞克提供。

Biljana Ciric: *A History of Exhibitions:
Shanghai 1979-2006*, Manchester's Centre
for Chinese Contemporary Art (CFCCA),
2014. All images in this lecture review are
courtesy of Biljana Ciric unless otherwise
specified.

国曼彻斯特华人艺术中心于2014年进行了出版发行。对于本地展览历史的长期关注和研究是我的个人选择，也和我开始策展之初的自身经历以及所处环境紧密相关。2000年我在中国修完硕士学位随即开始工作，对于艺术家自我组织的展览的研究兴趣以及一些当时所谓的"地下"展览对我产生的巨大影响促使我走上策展的道路。尽管在此之前我从未学习过任何策展课程，然而随着实践的深入，我意识到一种艺术上的休戚与共以及紧迫感：通过策展研究展览历史，并激活历史。但是我在一开始的时候也提到了，2000年时我所身处的艺术系统、面对的工作条件与当下是非常不同的。很多展览没有任何经济资助，就在仓库或半私人的场所而非艺术机构空间内举办。

研究自1976年"文化大革命"结束至2006年间艺术家在上海自我组织的展览和这段历史，对我这样一位积极实践的策展人来说是一个学习过程，我借此机会了解本土语境和同行的策展工作。我意识到切实保存这些档案的紧迫性，于是我尽可能地采访了仍在上海的、这段历史中的关键人物。在我将这段历史收录在我的档案和书籍中以前，这些展览几乎没有得到任何文献记载，也没有被纳入学校的课程。2009年，我自发启动了这个档案整理项目，并进行了三十余次艺术家采访。我们花了很多时间讨论当时这些展览是如何进行的，并重新绘制了平面图。我越来越意识到保存和激活这些被忽略的策展知识的重要性。

当时的西方艺术世界开始意识到对展览历史的研究梳理很大程度上决定了艺术史在当下的书写和论述，展览史逐渐成为一门重要的学科。然而，这种展览史的书写所天生持有的西方眼光，对我这样一位来自前南斯拉夫、选择在中国工作的塞尔维亚人而言，正是问题所在。在这样一种主流展览史的书写中，你无论如何都找不到中国展览史、上海展览史的身影，因此在那个当下身处本土语境之中的我确实油然而生一种强烈的个人意愿和使命感：我

1979年1月底至2月初《十二人画展》在上海黄浦区少年宫开幕

《十二人画展》在上海开幕

2. "十二人画展"展览现场，上海　　Exhibition view of "Twelve-Man Painting
黄浦区少年宫，1979。　　　　　Exhibition", Youth Palace of Huangpu
District, Shanghai, 1979.

希望通过编写此类关注本土展览史的图书档案，将西方主导的叙事往多元化和复杂化的方向推进，从而促进全球艺术的发展。

在《上海展览史 1979—2006》一书中，我尽可能收录了 1979 年至 2006 年间在上海举办的所有艺术家组织的展览相关的档案及文献，起始和结束的两个年份分别标识了上海展览史上第一个由艺术家独立发起组织的展览"十二人画展"的举办和以"38 个个展"为节点的这种艺术家自发组织展览的潮流的式微。理解这段历史的前提是我们必须清楚地认识到，早在美术馆一类的艺术机构尚未全面兴起的年代，这些由艺术家自发组织的展览便已开始积极地进行知识生产。我在刚开始研究整个上海展览史的时候，也关注了包括 1996 年第一届上海双年展在内的许多展览类型，但我发现其中最脆弱的还是艺术家组织的展览的历史，由于没有保存这些展览档案的物理空间和主观意识，很多原始资料都已经缺失了，这愈发引我感觉到作为策展人通过策展实践去保存、激活这段历史的紧迫性。

不得不说这项工作开展得很艰难——直到今日，展览史在中国以及亚洲的其他地区仍未被当作一个学术主题或学科来对待。但我的工作风格是一旦意识到做某件事的紧迫性，我就会排除万难，主动地去创造条件来完成它。我用了将近 5 年的时间，在胡昀、高铭研、唐狄鑫这几位艺术家朋友的协助下对当时参与展览的艺术家们进行了采访拍摄，自行完成了"上海展览史：1979 —2006"艺术项目。对当代艺术史的梳理和回顾方式有很多种，我选择的是类似艺术家钱喂康所言的一种"重现犯罪现场"的方法——尽可能去保存一手资料，而不在里面添加过多的主观判断和个人意见。

1979 年至 2006 年间在上海举办的这些艺术家组织的展览大都展期很短，展览发生的地点也各不相同，几乎都是非"白盒子"

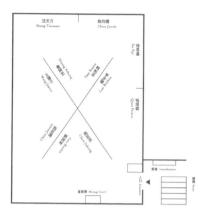

3. 艺术家陈巨源根据回忆重新绘制的"十二人画展"展览平面图。

The floor plan of "Twelve-Man Painting Exhibition" reproduced by artist Chen Juyuan from memory.

4. "38个个展"展览海报及展览现场，2006年。

Exhibition poster and installation view of "38 Solo Exhibitions", 2006.

空间，包括少年宫、教室、车库、电影院、咖啡厅等等。我们来看书内收录的两个具体的例子。1979年在黄浦区少年宫举办的"十二人画展"^{图示2, P6}是上海展览史上第一个由艺术家自行发起并独立组织的展览活动，它的重要性和1979年在北京举办的"星星美展"不相上下。它也是上海这段近30年的展览历史上展期最长、参观人数最多的展览，根据我对相关人士的采访得知，展览当年吸引了近2000人前来参观——尽管展出的作品仍然是非常传统的油画或水彩画，但此时的时代背景仍是"文化大革命"刚刚结束不久。这些早期的展览所留存下来的视觉材料有限，几乎只有一些模糊不清的现场照片，因此在我的研究工作里很关键的一步就是通过重制展览平面图来还原展览的面貌。事实上，很多类似"十二人画展"这样的早期展览是不存在原始的展览平面图的，布展的过程也很简单，艺术家会直接将作品摆放到空间内或挂到展墙上。重制平面图的作用是将展览的"身体经验"存档^{图示3, P8}。这一过程我会和艺术家们共同合作完成，通过回忆展览空间的样貌和展览呈现的状态，来还原一个尽量客观真实的展览平面图。由于参展艺术家们的回忆会掺杂许多主观因素，而时间久远也会导致记忆出现偏差，所以整个厘清事实和还原真相的过程往往会比较漫长。除此之外，艺术家采访也是我的工作方法之一，我会通过采访来了解展览发生的背景，包括当年他们是如何获得展览空间的使用以及资金来源等细节。当然并不是说采访过后所有的资料或相关内容会马上对外进行发表或出版成书，但是采访对我的策展工作而言是一种重要的建立并储存档案的方式。

我们再来看一下《上海展览史1979—2006》这本书中收录的最后一个展览"38个个展"^{图示4, P8}。为什么选择这个展览作为结篇？因为它标志了由策展人主导策划的展览模式兴起前，艺术家以展览为工具、为媒介所展开的艺术实验和形式探索上所作的最终尝试。

二十世纪90年代末涌现了以徐震、杨振中、杨福东等艺术家为代表的一代，他们围绕展览制造进行的一系列实验性探索曾深深启发了我，包括2002年的"范明珍和范明珠，孪生艺术展"、2004年的"62761232快递展"。当年这些展览受到的指摘是形式大过内容，也就是说艺术家对于展览形式的发明盖过了展览中展出作品的意义，展览本身成为了艺术家创作的一种艺术形式而被记住，而展出的作品并没有那么重要。于是，为了回应这种批评的声音，2006年由一群艺术家策划组织了"38个个展"。当时，美术馆基础建设在上海刚刚起步，这个大规模的展览获得了包括我当时任职的多伦美术馆在内的多个艺术机构的支持（这也是当年特有的一种集合不同力量紧密合作的方式），但是展览发生的地点选择在一个创意园区里的非艺术机构空间内。"38个个展"在开幕当天即被关停，展览现场的电闸被拉下，两位参展艺术家被逮捕。这个展览标志着艺术家自发组织展览的时代落下帷幕。此后，随着大批美术馆和当代艺术机构的集中涌现，以及商业因素对于整个艺术行业的不断介入，最终影响了作品的组织和展示方式朝着各种不同的可能性发展，艺术家们也开始真正回归到艺术家的职业角色中，结束了这一艺术家自主组织展览的传统。

以上大致介绍了我关于本土展览史的研究是如何活化成策展知识生产的。上海展览史的相关研究于2014年收尾，在出版这本书的同期，我还策划了一个展览"正如金钱不过纸造，展览也就是几间房"，不是用常规的文献展去呈现历史，而是通过委任创作的方式去激活文献。在这个展览里，以1979年至2006年间在上海举行、由艺术家组织的展览为背景，我邀请了多位本地及海外的艺术家就此段时期的展览文献资料展开创作与讨论，并与当下建立联系。

东南亚、中国、西方及其他

从2007、2008年开始，我将自己基于展览历史的研究范围扩大，关注中国本土的实践之余也放眼东南亚地区。东南亚当代艺术的发展包括艺术基建的运作方式和中国极其相似，但在当时鲜少有人将这二者之间建立联系，我决定同时沿着这两条脉络继续展开我的策展工作。

2008年，我策划了自己第一个关于东南亚地区的展览"在野策略——越南与柬埔寨当代文化现状"，展览的背景基于我对东南亚地域的当代文化艺术发展状态所进行的为期两年的研究图示5，P12。展览在曾经的可当代艺术中心举办，展出的大部分作品都是特定场域作品，我们看到的这件是柬埔寨艺术家 Sopheap Pich 的装置作品。2010年，我又与策展人 Jim Supangkat 共同策划了展览"当代性：印度尼西亚的当代艺术"，聚焦印度尼西亚的当代艺术实践及电影制作图示6，P12。除了常规的画册之外，我们为这两个展览都分别制作了读本，以便更好地向本地观众引入相关地域的背景介绍。

2012年是我关于东南亚地区的研究与策展工作的一个重要节点，在这一年我参与了由古根海姆美术馆联合瑞银集团(UBS)发起的一个全球艺术计划 MAP，并发表了文章《关于这个世界，艺术能告诉我们什么？东南亚、中国、西方及其他》，古根海姆美术馆对文章进行了中文翻译，感兴趣的朋友可以自行在其官网上阅读。从2012年到2018年，MAP 计划连续六年聚焦南亚及东南亚、拉丁美洲、中东及北非三个地区，通过发起策展人驻馆计划、国际巡展和作品收藏来促进全球范围内对"非代表性"地区当代艺术的关注。

5. "在野策略——越南与柬埔寨当代文化现状"展览现场，右图为柬埔寨艺术家 Sopheap Pich 的装置作品，可当代艺术中心，上海，2008年。

Exhibition view of "Strategies from Within: An Exhibition of Vietnamese and Cambodian Contemporary Art Practices", and the installation work (right) by Cambodian artist Sopheap Pich, Ke Center for the Contemporary Arts, Shanghai, 2008.

6. "当代性：印度尼西亚的当代艺术"展览现场，上海当代艺术馆，2010年。

Exhibition view of "Contemporaneity: Contemporary Art in Indonesia", MoCA Shanghai, 2010.

MAP 计划每届会为三个地区分别选出一位策展人，在古根海姆美术馆驻馆两年，策划一个关于该地区的展览，其中的大部分作品会被美术馆购入馆藏，以丰富古根海姆藏品构成的多样性。我是当年入围南亚及东南亚区域展的五位策展人之一，最后获选的是我的同事 June Yap。这段经验对我而言最有意义的地方在于，我由此了解到艺术机构是如何通过策展实践和展览制作来认知并关注边缘地区当代艺术现状及其发展的。

我最后一个有关东南亚地区的策展实践是 2011 年在曼彻斯特举办的展览"未来的机构"，作为当年亚洲三年展的展览项目呈现图示7, P13。当时整个欧洲都笼罩在自 2010 年开始的债务危机的阴影之下，而东南亚地区的艺术生产模式与自身文化中所蕴含的"团结"的概念密不可分，我认为这种工作模式或许可以为当时的欧洲困境提供一种别样的参考与借鉴。印尼艺术家团体 Ruangrupa 的作品就是一个很好的例子，他们制作了一份类似菜单的手册，题为《如何生存》。顺带一提，Ruangrupa 小组即将成为第十五届卡塞尔文献展的策展人，这也将是卡塞尔文献展历史上首次启用亚洲艺术家团体担任策展人。

这是我们在展览结束后制作的出版物。我个人的工作风格是极少会为所策划的展览出版画册，因为我觉得书籍本身就足以成为展览之外的延伸媒介。因此，在"未来的机构"展览结束之后，我决定策划一本同名出版物，以书为平台邀请了国际艺术家、策展人、评论家共同参与写作，一同为"未来的机构"畅想献计献策图示8, P13。

从展览的历史到展览制造的未来

2013 年是一个很特别的年份，整个中国、以及整个东南亚地区的艺术环境在短时间内迅速发生了变化：HUGO BOSS 亚洲新

7. "未来的机构"展览现场,图为艺术家团体 Ruangrupa 的作品展示区域,曼彻斯特华人艺术中心,2011 年。

Exhibition view of "Institution for the Future", CFCCA, 2011. The picture shows the area where the work by the art group Ruangrupa is displayed.

8. 《未来的机构》由比利安娜·思瑞克与 Sally Lai 共同主编,曼彻斯特华人艺术中心 2012 年出版。

Institution for the Future co-edited by Biljana Ciric and Sally Lai, published by CFCCA, 2012.

锐艺术家大奖创办，我很荣幸成为了首届评委会的一员；这一年，广州三年展首次关注了东南亚地区相关的议题；同时，我们也看到商业因素正在积极影响着语境的扩大。要成为一位独立策展人，每天都在面临的一个问题就是如何在一个不断变化的艺术系统和环境里明确自我定位并不断开展实践。当然，在这样一个系统里，作为策展人，你可以找到很多种不同的定位，但是中国本土的语境往往会在很短的时间内发生翻天覆地的变化，而你必须时刻对环境和工作条件发生的变化保持警醒，并从策展人的身份出发作出切实的回应。这就要求了策展人的工作方式和自我定位保持动态，时刻准备应对新的变化。随着2013年整个中国、以及整个东南亚地区艺术环境的变化，我对于策展的理解和自我定位也发生着转变——我开始思考过去是否投入了太多精力在制作展览上？我一度感觉到非常沮丧和迷茫，似乎一直以来所做的工作只是成为源源不断消耗着的、大量的艺术实践中的一部分。我重新思考了在这样一种不断变化的语境下该如何展开有效的工作。从那时起，我将自己生产展览的工作周期拉得非常长，花一两年的时间来做一个策展项目，思考这种"缓慢"生成不同形式的知识生产的可能。

这种慢节奏之下，我对策展工作的理解以及对展览的思考方式产生了变化，成果之一就是我近期完成的《从展览的历史到展览制造的未来：中国与东南亚》一书。我先前提到了，展览史长期以来就是我展开策展实践的一个重要母题。在我开始进行上海展览史研究的时候，我其实是非常孤独的。当时在这个领域里只有我一个人，工作开展得很艰难，哪怕到了今天，我仍有孤军作战之感。我非常希望年轻一代的策展人可以展开关于其他类型或类别的展览史研究，我也非常希望通过拓展与本地同行的合作，共同为中国以及东南亚地区的展览历史建立档案。当然，要达成这个目标须得创造非常实际的、有机的工作条件，另外，很重要的一点，研究的开展和档案的生产与建立需要充足的时间积淀。

9. "从展览的历史到展览制造的未来"项目第一次研讨会的资料，奥克兰 St Paul Street Gallery，2013年。

Documents of the first assembly of "From A History of Exhibitions Towards the Future of Exhibition Making", St Paul Street Gallery, Auckland, 2013.

10. "阅览室"现场，上海外滩美术馆，2018年。
图片致谢：上海外滩美术馆。

On-site scene of the "Reading Room", Rockbund Art Museum, Shanghai, 2018. Courtesy of Rockbund Art Museum, Shanghai.

基于上述思考，我开始了"从展览的历史到展览制造的未来"这一长期研究项目。这个项目的基本工作框架是由一系列发生在不同地点的研讨会循序推进的，研讨会每隔几年召开，每次的间隔期就是新的研究不断开展和落地的过程。最终收录到出版物内的所有研究成果都是最前沿的，因为在这一领域里并没有任何前人已完成的文献研究成果可供引用或直接收录。另外很重要的一点是研究者们对于所研究地域的语境需要有充分且深入的认知，才能有效地建立起对话和交流，而作为出版物的主编，我更是需要充分理解这些背景，才能与同事们在收录展览之时有所判断。

第一次集会 2013 年在新西兰举行，研讨会发生的地点在奥克兰一所大学设立的美术馆 St Paul Street Gallery，这次研讨会也是由侯瀚如策展的第五届奥克兰三年展的公共项目^{图示9，P16}。每一次的集会都会设立一个特定时间范围内的研究主题，唯一的特例是第一次研讨会。由于当时我们放眼于不同地区早期的前卫展览实践，因此很难在时间线索上达成一个统一而明确的时代框架，比如越南早期的展览探索集中于 1980 年代末期至 1990 年代初期，而中国的语境则始于 1980 年代初。因此第一次的研讨会是笼统地围绕早期展览实践的个案研究展开的。

第二次集会于 2018 年在上海外滩美术馆举行，这一次的研讨会主题为"1990 年代中国及东南亚地区的策展实践"，距离第一次集会已过去了 5 年。在这里提到这个时间跨度，是因为我特别想再强调，我们真的要为策展实践和前期研究工作留足时间空间。这次集会讨论了中国及亚洲地区在二十世纪 90 年代开展的一系列当代艺术探索中的代表性案例。从本次集会开始，我们有几大创举：一是设立了专项研究基金，用以支持研究展览史的年轻人；二是在合作的美术馆内设立了展览史研究专题阅览室^{图示10，P16}，以便与更多观众分享研究者收集的文献资料以及与课题相关的书籍；三是在研讨会召开前便提前开展了一系列公共活动，致力于向公众分享研究者工作的最新进展，让大家意识到这是一个正在发生的、持续进行的研究项目图示11, P20。

研讨会系列的最后一次集会于2019年底在广东时代美术馆举办，这一次的主题聚焦2000年后中国和东南亚地区的策展实践。我经常半开玩笑地说，为什么现如今全世界的展览都长得一模一样？策展人到底做了什么？因此，本次的研讨会的核心正是要去关注这种展览越来越标准化、双年展模式盛行的现象，并探讨我们如何通过区域研究抛出不同的策展思路，以突出重围。除了继续设立专项基金支持年轻研究员之外，本次集会也延续了第二次集会时启用的"阅览室"项目，但是在形式上进行了创新。我邀请了来自武汉的年轻艺术家程婷婷介入阅览室的展陈设计，同时也在阅读空间内展示了她的自画像、小型雕塑等作品。此外，我也邀请她从性别观点的角度出发，基于阅览室内展出的文献和档案创作一系列新作品，这些作品会在阅览室项目的最后阶段在空间内呈现图示12, P21。

最后回到出版物《从展览的历史到展览制造的未来：中国与东南亚》，书内收录的研究论文都是经由提前约稿或征集所得，最终收录了近20位作者的重要研究成果图示13, P22。本书邀请了泰国艺术家Pratchaya Phinthong参与设计，当读者翻开这本书的时候或许会注意到有些页面是有折角的，这正是艺术家的创意。本书内提到的很多展览虽然大都是由艺术家自发组织策划的，然而这些展览历史的书写者往往是策展人或评论家，人们似乎已经习惯忽略艺术家的声音。

因此我找来了艺术家介入本书的"创作"，希望藉由设计向读者提示艺术家在这些知识生产中的重要性，重视这些容易被忽略的声音。Pratchaya在这里也延续了他挑战策展人的习惯——他把决定具体在哪一页做折角的选择权交到了我编辑手里。有趣的是，几天前我带着这本书去米兰新美术学院(NABA)交流，院长很好奇地指着其中有折角的一页问我为什么选择这页？是因为它的内容是书中最重要的吗？我回答说不，这是这本书内的艺术家项目，而选择这几页做折角只是为了纪念我最近失去的一位重要的艺术家朋友 Roslisham Ismail Aka Ise，有折角的页码暗合了他的人生经历。当我刚开始做东南亚地区展览史研究的时候，筚路蓝缕，正是 Ise 慷慨地借出他的房子供我们在地调研时居住。他曾笑言自己的房子是"停车场"，朋友们来了一拨又一拨，每一次他都会热心地招待并充当向导。我想借由这个小小的举动来缅怀这位挚友，并表达我的敬意。

我的分享就到这里，谢谢大家！ ∎

11. 在第二次研讨会前开展的部分公共活动的海报，从左到右依次为："寻迹山火"，"展览再现：'肌肤三部曲'时间、空间及社群研究"，"目击成长：喻红1990年代以来的艺术实践"，"展览史研究：亚洲当代艺术的关键挑战"，上海外滩美术馆，2018年。

From left to right, posters of some public events held before the second assembly, i.e. "Inching Towards the Fire"; "Performing the Exhibition: The Investigation of Time, Space and Community in the Skin Trilogy"; "Witness to Growth: Yu Hong's Artistic Practices From the 1990s to Today"; "Researching on Exhibition Histories: A Decisive Challenge for Contemporary Art in Asia", Rockbund Art Museum, Shanghai, 2018.

12. 第二期"阅览室"现场，广东时
　　代美术馆，2019年。
　　图片致谢：广东时代美术馆。

Installation view of "Reading Room",
Guangdong Times Museum, 2019.
Courtesy of Guangdong Times Museum.

13. 比丽安娜·思瑞克主编《从展览的历史到展览制造的未来：中国与东南亚》，2020 年由 Sternberg 出版社联合广东时代美术馆、上海外滩美术馆、奥克兰 St Paul Street Gallery 共同出版。

From a History of Exhibitions Towards a Future of Exhibition-Making: China and Southeast Asia, edited by Biljana Ciric, co-published by Sternberg Press, Guangdong Times Museum, Rockbund Art Museum, and St Paul Street Gallery.

Independent curator Biljana Ciric's presentation is situated around the notion of curating and her curatorial practice in China. In the last nearly twenty years, Ciric has been committed to the history of exhibitions in the local context. The presentation takes her research of artist-organized exhibitions in Shanghai between 1979 and 2006 as a point of departure, and continues with the exploration of different forms of knowledge production beyond exhibition. Ciric explains her working methodology and notion of curating through a series of study cases.

Biljana Ciric: Curating and its Urgencies

I would like to thank PSA for its invitation. In the beginning, I asked you two practical questions: What do you do? What do you live on? I started my curatorial practice in Shanghai around 2000, since when the general environment and working conditions for young curators have changed greatly. Therefore, I am interested in how you deal with the reality on the practical level. Today I am going to focus on a series of my curatorial practice in China—how the local context constitutes my curatorial work and how that very context formed my understanding of curating.

Curatorial Practice Based on the Research on the History of Exhibitions in Shanghai: Revisiting, Activating and Producing knowledge

In 2013, I initiated a long-term research project on China and Southeast Asia, "From a History of Exhibitions Towards a Future of Exhibition-Making: China and Southeast Asia". The project recently ended with the final assembly and the publishing of a namesake book on the research results. The assembly re-examines the importance of exhibitions as a form and medium, and discusses the importance of artist-organized exhibitions in a local context in different localities by engaging writers, curators and art professionals to create archives around certain exhibitions. I will come back to the development of this project in the last part of my presentation. In 2014, I compiled the book, *A History of Exhibitions: Shanghai 1979–2006* Fig. 1, P4, which is an archive of artist-organized exhibitions in Shanghai from 1979 to 2006. The book was published by the Centre for Chinese Contemporary Art (CFCCA). My long-term dedication to and research on the history of local exhibitions is a choice of mine, and also a result of my personal curatorial experience and the art environment at the time. In 2000, I started to work right after the completion of my postgraduate study in China. I set out on curatorial practice, as a result of my encounter of artist-organized exhibitions and the great impact left on me by some of these then underground exhibitions in early 2000. Although I had not taken any curatorial courses, I developed a sense of artistic solidarity and urgency that I shall study and activate the history of exhibitions through my curatorial practice. However, as I have mentioned at first, the art system and working conditions in early 2000 were very different from what we see today. Many exhibitions were held in warehouses or semi-private settings instead of institutional spaces, with no financial support of any kind.

Doing research on artist-organized exhibitions in Shanghai from the end of the Cultural Revolution in 1976 to 2006 was a learning process for me as an active curator to understand the local context and curatorial work of my peers. It was also urgent to preserve these archives, so I tried to interview some of the key figures that were still around. Besides my own archive and book, these exhibitions stay very much undocumented and out of the curriculum. In 2009, I initiated this archiving project on my own and conducted over 30 interviews with artists. I spent much time with them discussing how these exhibitions came about and re-making the floor plans. I become more and more aware that the curatorial knowledge that went overlooked has to be preserved and activated.

The Western art system in the last ten or more years starts to see exhibition histories as an academic field and realizes that the very knowledge shapes greatly how art history is written and discussed today. Of course, it is still very problematic that most of the well archived and discussed exhibitions are the ones in the West, while exhibitions on artistic practice or different working methods in the rest of the world stay largely unidentified and unknown to world. Being a curator informed by the local context in China and a Serbian growing up in the former Yugoslavia, it is a very frustrating fact for me that the history of exhibitions in Shanghai or China is nowhere to be found in the mainstream exhibition history. That is why I developed a strong will and a sense of responsibility in the local context at that time. My hope is that the compilation of such a locally initiated research can diversify and enrich the Western-dominated narrative so as to contribute to the global art world.

In the book *A History of Exhibitions: Shanghai 1979–2006*, I collected as many archives and documents on artist-organized exhibitions in Shanghai from 1979 to 2006 as possible. The first and last years of this period indicate the opening of the first artist-organized exhibition in Shanghai, "Twelve-Man Painting Exhibition" and the decline of artist-organized exhibitions marked by "38 Solo Exhibitions", respectively. To understand the history during this period, we must be clear that before art museums and institutions went into full swing, artist-organized exhibitions already began to actively produce knowledge. When I studied the history of exhibitions in Shanghai, I also paid attention to many different exhibitions, including the first Shanghai Biennale in 1996. I found that the most vulnerable are artist-organized exhibitions. Many of the original materials are lost due to the lack of physical space and subjective awareness of preserving exhibition archives, which increasingly urged me to preserve and activate this history through my curatorial practice.

I have to say that it is hard work—even today, exhibition history is not treated as an academic topic or field yet in China nor in the rest of Asia. Nevertheless, my curatorial work is usually framed around the urgency that I need to address, and if it is urgent to do something, I will somehow create conditions to do it. I spent 5 years interviewing artists who participated in these exhibitions and documenting all these interviews in the video format with the help of my artist friends, Hu Yun, Gao Mingyan and Tang Dixin. After the interviews, I completed the project, "A History of Exhibitions: Shanghai 1979–2006", totally on my own. There are many methodologies to study and review the history of contemporary art, and the one

I felt most comfortable with is similar to what is called by artist Qian Weikang, "recreating the crime scenes", namely, try to preserve as many primary resources and materials as possible without excessive subjective judgment or personal opinions.

Exhibitions organized by artists in Shanghai from 1979 to 2006 mostly were very short and held in different places, almost all in "non-white cube" spaces, such as youth palace, classroom, garage, cinema and cafe. Here are two examples from the book. The "Twelve-Man Painting Exhibition" held in the Youth Palace of Huangpu District in 1979 was the first event self-initiated and independently organized exhibition by artists in the exhibition history of Shanghai ^{Fig. 2, P6}, with a comparable importance to the "Star Art Exhibition" in Beijing in 1979. It is the longest and most-visited exhibition in Shanghai's exhibition history in the last thirty years. According to the people I interviewed, the exhibition attracted nearly 2,000 viewers that year. It featured very traditional oil paintings or watercolors, but we should see that it was held right after the end of the Cultural Revolution. Only a few visual materials have been retained from these early exhibitions, and the photos of the installation views are not clear. Therefore, a key step in my research work is to restore the exhibitions by remaking the floor plans. In fact, many of these early exhibitions like the "Twelve-Man Painting Exhibition" had no floor plan, and artists simply brought in the works and put things on the wall or in the room. Through the floorplan, I tried to preserve the "physicality" of exhibition, as part of the archive ^{Fig. 3, P6}. By recalling how the space and the exhibition looked like, I worked together with the artists to re-draw the floorplan as objective and as true as possible. Due to the subjectivity of private memories and the difficulties in remembering every detail precisely after so many years, the entire process of restoring the facts is relatively longer than usual. Besides, artist interview is another working methodology of mine. I interviewed artists to understand the background of the exhibitions, including how they found the exhibition space and sourced the funds. Not all materials or related contents would be published in a book right after the interviews, but interview is still an important method to create documentations and form archives for my curatorial practice.

The last exhibition in the book *A History of Exhibitions: Shanghai 1979–2006* is called "38 Solo Exhibitions" Fig. 4, P8. The book is concluded with this exhibition, because it marks the final attempt of the last generation of artists who used exhibitions as the tool and medium for artistic experiment and formal exploration, before the rise of curator-organized exhibitions.

In the late 1990s, there was a generation of artists like Xu Zhen, Yang Zhenzhong, and Yang Fudong. They started experimenting with exhibition-making, which inspired me deeply. For example, "FAN Mingzhen and FAN Mingzhu: Glad to Meet You, Twin Exhibition" in 2002, and "DIAL 62761232" in 2004. At that time, these exhibitions were criticized by art community for paying more attention to the form and method than to the content. That is to say, the exhibition form appeared much stronger than art works, so that the exhibition itself was remembered as a creation, while the works on site became less important. In response to this criticism, a group of artists curated "38 Solo Exhibitions" in 2006. Back then, art infrastructure like museums just emerged in Shanghai. The making of this large-scale exhibition was supported by many different art institutions, including Duolun Museum of Modern Art where I worked, which was a unique way in that period how various communities work closely together. However, the exhibition was not held in an art institution but in a creative industry park. "38 Solo Exhibitions" was closed at the opening. Electricity was cut off, and two artists were arrested. This exhibition marks the end of era of the artist-organized exhibitions. Since then, slowly with the rise of museums and institutions of contemporary art as well as the increasing influence of commercial factors throughout the art industry, the organization and display of artworks have been driven towards all different possibilities. Meanwhile, artists really started to perceive and return to their professional roles of being artists, bringing the tradition of artist-organized exhibitions to an end.

This is the background about how I think about the exhibition history and how this becomes my active curatorial knowledge. I completed the research on the exhibition history of Shanghai in 2014. While working on the publishing of the book, I curated an exhibition, "Just Like Money is Made of Paper, The Gallery is The Room". Instead of presenting the history by showcasing historical documents, I tried to activate the archives through artist commissions. Thus, I collaborated with a group of local and international artists, and invited them to discuss and work on those archives as a point of departure, trying to find relevant connections to our current moment in time.

Southeast Asia, China, the West and the Rest

Since 2007 and 2008, I began to extend my research interest based on exhibition history. In parallel to my work in China, I started a research on Southeast Asia. The development of contemporary art in Southeast Asia, including the way art infrastructure work, is very similar to that in China, but there were few connections between the two at that point.

In 2008, I curated my first exhibition on Southeast Asia, "Strategies from Within: An Exhibition of Vietnamese and Cambodian Contemporary Art Practices", based on my two-year research on the development of contemporary culture and art in this area [Fig. 5, P12]. The exhibition was held in Ke Center for the Contemporary Arts, and most of the works on show were site-specific. For example, this is an installation by Cambodian artist Sopheap Pich shown at the exhibition. In 2010 during Shanghai World Expo, I co-curated the exhibition "Contemporaneity: Contemporary Art in Indonesia" with the curator Jim Supangkat, focusing on contemporary art and film-making practice in Indonesia [Fig. 6, P12]. In addition to exhibition catalogs, we also made readers for the two exhibitions, respectively, introducing the contexts to the local audience.

The year of 2012 is essential to my research and curatorial work on Southeast Asia, when I participated in the MAP Global Art Initiative co-founded by the Guggenheim Museum and the UBS, publishing an article titled "What Can Art Tell Us About This World? Southeast Asia, China, the West, and the Rest". The Guggenheim Museum have this article translated in Chinese, and those who are interested in can read the text on the museum's website. From 2012 to 2018, MAP focused on South and Southeast Asia, Latin America, the Middle East, and North Africa for six consecutive years, and increased the global attention to "under-represented" regional contemporary art through the residency program, international travelling exhibitions, and artwork collection.

For each edition, MAP invites one curator from each of the three geographic regions to attend a two-year curatorial residency at the Guggenheim Museum and curate an exhibition about the region. Most of the works will be purchased by the Museum to diversify its collection. I was one of the five curators who was shortlisted for the exhibition on South and Southeast Asia, and my colleague June Yap was selected. For me, it is a very interesting experience to understand how art institutions perceive and pay attention to the current situation and development of contemporary art in marginal localities through curatorial practice and exhibition-making.

The last curatorial practice that I actively engaged with the region of Southeast Asia is the exhibition called "Institution for the Future" in Manchester in 2011, which was also presented as part of the Asian Triennial that very year [Fig. 7, P13]. At that time, the shadow of the debt crisis since 2010 shrouded throughout Europe. Understanding the art production mode in Southeast Asia which is very much related to the notion of "solidarity" embedded in its native culture, I regard it as a unique reference to think differently about the situation in Europe. The work by the Indonesian art group Ruangrupa is a good example. They made a menu-like manual, *How to Survive*. Incidentally, Ruangrupa is going to be the curator of Documenta 15 in Kassel. It will be the first time that an Asian art group is appointed as the curator in the history of Documenta.

This is the final publication after the exhibition. I rarely publish any catalog for the exhibitions I curate, because it is not the way I work, and I do think books themselves are sufficient as an extended medium of exhibitions. Therefore, after this exhibition, I decided to produce a namesake book, inviting international artists, curators, and critics to jointly participate in the writing and contribute ideas to the vision of Institution for the Future[Fig. 8, P13].

From a History of Exhibitions Towards the Future of Exhibition Making

The year of 2013 is critical, witnessing how rapidly the context in China, as well as in the whole Southeast Asia changed in a short period of time. In 2013, the HUGO BOSS ASIA ART Award for emerging Asian artists was founded, and I was honored to join the first jury. In the same year, the Guangzhou Triennial paid attention to issues related to Southeast Asia for the first time. Meanwhile, commercial factors also started to get actively engaged in the expansion of context. Being an independent curator like, this is what one has to deal with in his/her work, that is, to position him/herself and keep the position dynamic in such a constantly changing art system and environment. Of course, there are different positions you can take on, but the local context in China can change drastically over a short period of time. Therefore, one must be highly aware of the changes to the environment and working conditions at all times, and make a substantial response as a curator. This requires curators to maintain a dynamic work style and position and to be well prepared to respond to new changes. With the changes in the context of China and Southeast Asia in 2013, my notion of curating and my positioning also changed—I began to think about if I had devoted too much in making exhibitions. I was very depressed and lost, because I felt that my work was only a fraction and just contributed to the consumption of art practice. I had to rethink how to work effectively within such a constantly changing context. From that point on, my exhibition-making process became very long. I started doing one-year or two-year exhibitions, thinking about the notion of slowness and how it can produce different formats of knowledge.

As a response to this thinking, my perception of curatorial work and way of making exhibition really changed. The newly-published book *From A History of Exhibitions Towards the Future of Exhibition Making: China and Southeast Asia*, is one of the outcomes related to my change. As I mentioned earlier, exhibition history has long been a motif of my curatorial practice. When I started the research on the exhibition history in Shanghai, I was all by myself in what I did, and it was no easy work. Even today, I feel that I am still the only one. I very much hope that the younger generation of curators can do further research on other types or categories of exhibition history, and I also hope to expand my research, working with my peers in the region to jointly produce archives for exhibition history in China and in Southeast Asia. For sure, it is necessary to create practical and organic working conditions in order to achieve this goal. It is also essential to allow adequate time for conducting research, producing documents and forming the archives.

Based on the above-mentioned thinking, I started the long-term research project, "From A History of Exhibitions Towards the Future of Exhibition Making". Essentially, this project is accumulatively promoted by a series of seminars that take place in a different location every few years. During each interval, new research keeps being conducted and completed. The articles in the academic publication of the project represent the most cutting-edge research results, because there is no ready document nor research result in the field by the predecessors that can be cited or directly included in this book. What is very important is that researchers should have a thorough and in-depth understanding of the local context in the region they study so that they can effectively establish a dialogue and communication. While as the chief editor of the book, I need to know well enough the local context of different regions in order to understand why a specific exhibition is entering the book and to make decisions when working with different colleagues.

The first assembly was held in St Paul Street Gallery—an art museum set up by a university in Auckland, New Zealand—in 2013. The assembly was also a public project of the 5th Auckland Triennial curated by Hou Hanru [Fig. 9, P16]. Each assembly was structured around a specific research theme within a certain time period, except for the first one. At that time, we were looking at the early avant-garde exhibitions in different localities, so it was difficult to reach a unified, clear time frame. For example, the early exploration on exhibition-making in Vietnam concentrated from the late 1980s to the early 1990s, while started in the early 1980s in China. Therefore, the first assembly was generally centered around the case study of early exhibition practice.

The second assembly was held at the Rockbund Art Museum, Shanghai in 2018, under the theme of "Curatorial Practices in China and Southeast Asia in the 1990s". It took five years to produce the second assembly after the first one. I am bringing up the time span, because I would like to re-emphasize here that you have to allow enough time for your curatorial practice and preliminary research. This assembly discussed representative cases of a series of explorations on contemporary art in China and elsewhere across Asia in the 1990s. We acquired a larger structure and made several innovations in this assembly. First, a research grant for young researchers who study exhibition history has been founded; second, a special reading room dedicated to exhibition history research was set up in our collaborated art museum, so as to share with a larger audience the archives collected by researchers and books related to the topics [Fig. 10, P16]; third, a series of public events were launched in advance of the seminar, to present the latest research work of our guest speakers and remind people that it is an ongoing research project [Fig. 11, P16].

The final assembly was held at Guangdong Times Museum, at the end of 2019, under the theme of "Curatorial Practice in China and Southeast Asia After 2000". There is a very basic question, which I always say as a joke: why exhibitions in the world all look the same today? What happened to us? Therefore, this assembly was held with a few focal points: the increasingly standardized exhibition-making practice, the prevalence of biennale modes, and how to generate different curatorial ideas through regional research and make a breakthrough. In addition to the special grant for young researchers, we continued the "Reading Room" project with a different form. I invited a young artist from Wuhan, Cheng Tingting, to work with me on the space design of the reading room. Some of Cheng's works including her self-portraits and small sculptures were displayed in the the reading room. In addition, I have invited her to create new works based on the documents and archives showcased in the "Reading Room" and from the gender perspective. These works will be presented in the space at the final stage of the "Reading Room" [Fig. 12, P18].

Finally, let's get back to the book, *A History of Exhibitions Towards the Future of Exhibition Making: China and Southeast Asia* [Fig. 13, P20]. The book includes papers on the key research results by twenty authors, all of which were either commissioned or obtained through advance submissions to the call-up. I invited Thai artist Pratchaya Phinthong to participate in the book design. When readers open this book, they may notice that some pages are flipped, which is the artist's idea. Although many of the exhibitions mentioned in this book were artist-organized, the exhibition history was mostly written by curators or critics. As a result, people seem to be used to ignoring the artists' voices.

Therefore, I engaged an artist in the "creation" of this book, acknowledging the importance of artists' existence in knowledge production and drawing attention to their easily overlooked voices. In this project, Pratchaya continued his habit of challenging the curator—he left it to me (the editor) to decide which page to be flipped over. It is interesting that when I took this book to the New Academy of Fine Arts (NABA) in Milan a few days ago, director of NABA Marco Scottini curiously pointed to one page and asked me why it is flipped and if it is one of the most important texts. I said no, and explained that it was an artist's project, and I chose these pages to pay homage to an important artist friend, Roslisham Ismail Aka Ise, who passed recently. The dates within the book symbolically related to his life. When I first started doing research on the exhibition history in Southeast Asia, we had no money and it was Ise who generously lent his house to us during our field research. He once jokingly said that his house was a "parking project" where friends came and parked. Whoever came, he would kindly host them and take them around. This little design within the book is my homage to this great friend Ise.

That's all for today. Thank you!

青策充电站

联合主办：上海当代艺术博物馆、复旦大学哲学学院

工作团队

上海当代艺术博物馆：张琍莉、马慧婷、徐辰斐、邱鼎、黄彦娜

复旦大学哲学学院：袁新、林晖、沈奇岚、陈佳

实录册编辑团队

编辑：马慧婷、蔺佳

平面设计：邵君瑜

翻译：曾晨

校对：阮汇善

ECP Charging Station Programme
Co-organizers: Power Station of Art,
School of Philosophy, Fudan University

Programme Team
Power Station of Art: Zhang Lili, Ma Huiting, Xu Chenfei,
Qiu Ding, Huang Yanna
School of Philosophy, Fudan University: Yuan Xin, Lin Hui,
Shen Qilan, Chen Jia

Editorial Team
Editor: Ma Huiting, Lin Jia
Graphic Design: Shao Junyu
Translator: Zen Chen
Proofreader: Ruan Huishan

"青策充电站"部分导师、学员与嘉宾
合影，上海当代艺术博物馆，2020
年1月。
© 上海当代艺术博物馆

Group photo of some of the lecturers,
participants and guests of the ECP
Charging Station Programme, Power
Station of Art, Shanghai, January 2020.
© Power Station of Art